THE REAL GREEK

THE REAL GREEK

EAT.HEALTHY.TOGETHER.

WITH
TONIA BUXTON

Photography by Vanessa Courtier

Food styling and recipe editing by Wendy Veale

BLINK
bringing you closer

Published by Blink Publishing
3.25, The Plaza,
535 Kings Road,
Chelsea Harbour,
London, SW10 0SZ

www.blinkpublishing.co.uk

facebook.com/blinkpublishing
twitter.com/blinkpublishing

HB 978-1-910536-95-7

A CIP catalogue of this book is available from the British Library.

Jacket design by Nathan Balsom
Design and typset by www.envydesign.co.uk
Printed in Italy

1 3 5 7 9 10 8 6 4 2

First published by Blink Publishing in 2016

Papers used by Blink Publishing are natural, recyclable products made from wood grown in sustainable forests. The manufacturing processes conform to the environmental regulations of the country of origin.

Every reasonable effort has been made to trace copyright holders of material reproduced in this book, but if any have been inadvertently overlooked the publishers would be glad to hear from them.

Blink Publishing is an imprint of the Bonnier Publishing Group
www.bonnierpublishing.co.uk

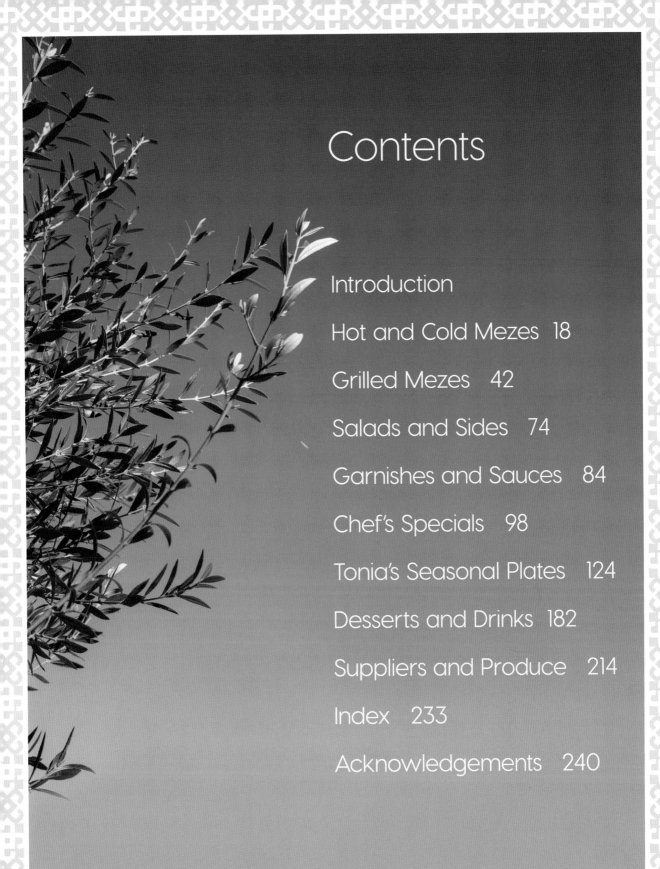

Contents

My Real Greek Story

Working with The Real Greek has been a dream for me. It encompasses all I love in life: food, authenticity, fun, drama and lots of eating!

For my whole career I have been extolling the benefits of Greek cuisine, not just how delicious it is, but also how good it can be for you. What other cuisine has such diversity? Greece takes in the traditions from her 6,000 islands, from the fertile mainlands all the way up to the highest mountains. What we try to do at The Real Greek is to bring you a taste of that.

From the moment I joined the team at The Real Greek, I was made to feel like family. I am constantly working with Nabil, Emily and Christos to try and evolve The Real Greek into the best restaurant it can be, and I think we are doing a pretty good job. It has been a pleasure for me to work on The Real Greek Cookbook, and I hope you enjoy cooking from it as much as I enjoyed collating it.

And, to quote my favourite philosopher Aristotle:
'Pleasure in the job puts perfection in the work.'

Nabil Mankarious

Growing up in Alexandria, I enjoyed eating food that I had always believed to be inherently Egyptian cuisine. However, I have since come to realise that the dishes I was brought up on had their roots in Greece. As well as having our own version of moussaka (sans meat), stuffed vine leaves and baked pasta dishes were also commonplace on our table and are known to the Greeks as *dolmades* and *pastitsio* respectively.

Alexandria has a long and well-established connection with Greece ever since it was founded by Alexander the Great in 332 BC. There is still a thriving Greek community in Alexandria, and I have fond memories of playing football in the Greek youth centre that was across from where I lived in Camp Caesar. Occasionally,

a few of the boys would invite me back to their homes afterwards for dinner with their families. To this day, whenever I visit Greece, I always seem to run into someone telling me of their relatives in Alexandria and asking if I know of them!

Since I have been involved with The Real Greek, we've changed the menu as well as the ingredients to connect all of our dishes to Alexander the Great's travels throughout the Eastern Mediterranean. I personally believe he managed to influence both Greek and Eastern Mediterranean cuisine by exchanging thoughts and ideas about food with the many cultures he encountered. Of course, there may have been many influences before and after Alexander the Great, but for me, he was the first.

Christos
Karatzenis

I've always thought that I was born to be a restaurateur. One path and one life, simple as that.

It helped that my father was the well-known "Jimmy of Kolonaki", a chef and restaurateur whose hands prepared food for politicians, celebrities and many other people for decades.

I took my first steps in the business back in the early eighties, when I was just 16 years old, in our family-owned restaurant in Loukianou. Years passed, almost 30 of them, with lots of new restaurants, awards and business ventures, when suddenly fate brought

me to London and The Real Greek. It became my passion, and allowed me to follow my Dad's dreams way before open borders in Europe made this more accessible.

Working alongside Nabil and a team of passionate people, we made it our mission to bring the tastes of Greece and the warm hospitality of Greek people to every Londoner and friend of The Real Greek. And when inspiration and ingredients are needed, our legendary research trips to every part of Greece have the solution! In the end, the most important thing is that everything has to be 'Real Greek!'.

Emily Douglas

I have been with The Real Greek since it started on its journey and, wow, what changes I have seen throughout these past 6 years!

I am so proud of the food that we serve and the people that we work with. It's a big family, all passionate and committed to what we do.

I don't speak Greek, but by being surrounded by Greek food, culture and the language on a daily basis, funnily enough I actually understand what is being said very well, which surprises a lot of people! I think it's because my heart is actually Greek.

Introducing Greek Food

My forefathers, the ancient Greeks, were the first to understand the complex need to mix foods together in a certain way to make them pleasing to the palate. It was Archestratus in 320 BC who wrote the first cookbook in history, in which he advises his readers on where to get the best food in the Mediterranean world. Greece has a culinary tradition thousands of years old and, as with so many things, we Greeks did it first before the rest of the world copied us.

Here at The Real Greek we have authenticity as our guide. Where we can, we like to keep it 'Real Greek'. We have the best olive oil from the ancient groves of Crete, the home of the world's oldest living olive tree. Over 3,000 years old and it is still producing olives!

Equally, our honey is the best in the world, hailing from the island of Ikaria renowned for the longevity of it's people. The land has not been polluted by large industry, so the honey is totally pure.

Our yoghurt comes from a farm in Attica, just outside Athens, and is made in the traditional Greek way, making it high in protein and creamy to taste.

The dishes on The Real Greek menu are from all over Greece; both the mountainous fertile mainland and the islands around her. Some are even inspired by the travels of Alexander the Great around Eastern Europe. Whether you are vegan, vegetarian, pescetarian or a meat-eater, there is so much variety in Greek cuisine. We have included the recipes that are on the menu, as well as seasonal specials and unique recipes from our chefs, staff and wider clan.

The Real Greek is a family and I am very honored to be part of it. I hope you enjoy our cookbook.

Hot and Cold Mezes

Dolmades

Serves 4 as Meze or Makes 20 Dolmades

250g long-grain or pudding rice
2 onions, finely chopped
1 Bird's eye chilli, deseeded and finely chopped
250g passata or 400g can chopped tomatoes
4 tbsp. finely chopped flat-leaf parsley
4 tbsp. finely chopped dill
2 tbsp. finely chopped mint leaves
250g fresh vine leaves, destalked (or use leaves in brine, drained)
Sea salt & freshly ground black pepper, to taste
A drizzle of extra virgin olive oil
2 lemons, cut in wedges

Dolmades are often served as part of the meze at wedding feasts in Greece - a great excuse for village women to meet up beforehand to roll hundreds of dolmades whilst catching up on local gossip!

In Cyprus we call dolmades 'koupepia', which means 'little cigars'.

- Bring 500ml water to the boil in a large saucepan, then add the rice with a good pinch of salt. Part-cover and reduce the heat to simmer for 12-15 minutes or until the rice is just starting to soften.

- Preheat the oven to 180°C (fan 160°C) / Gas 4.

- Drain the rice and leave to cool a little before mixing in the onion, chilli, passata and chopped herbs. Season well.

- Have a stack of the prepared vine leaves ready, vein-side facing up, the rice mixture and a shallow (preferably circular) ovenproof dish ready to put the dolmades in.

- To make a dolmade, place 1 tsp. of the mixture one third up from the centre base of a leaf, fold the leaf over the rice from the base, then fold in the left and right side of the leaf. Roll up the leaf to make a mini cigar shape.

- Continue until all the dolmades are made and tightly packed side by side in the dish. Squeeze over the lemon juice, then cover the dolmades with the remaining vine leaves.

- Place a plate, upside down on top of the vine leaves, then pour boiling water in around the edge of the dish to come up to just where it touches the plate. Cover with foil and transfer to the oven to cook for 30-40 minutes.

- Serve warm or cold with a drizzle of olive oil or Ladolemo (see page 87) and some lemon wedges.

Prawns with Feta and Ouzo

Serves 4–6

4 tbsp. olive oil

FOR THE SAUCE:
250g onions, chopped
4 cloves of garlic, chopped
4 tbsp. retsina or white wine
1 heaped tbsp. tomato purée
2 x 400g cans chopped
    tomatoes
1 tbsp. freshly chopped dill

1kg fresh raw tiger prawns,
    butterflied
4 tbsp. ouzo
150g feta cheese, cubed
1 lemon, cut into wedges
Sea salt and freshly ground
    black pepper, to taste

Finger-licking tiger prawns cooked in ouzo with softened feta cheese all in a rich thick tomato sauce. A little goes a long way when served Meze-style.

Delicious too as a main meal eaten with a Greek salad and crusty bread.

- Heat 2 tbsp. olive oil in a large frying pan. Gently cook the onions for 10 minutes or until softened but not coloured. Add the garlic, retsina, tomato purée, chopped tomatoes and 100ml water. Season with salt and pepper, cover and simmer for 30 minutes.

- Cool a little, then blitz with a hand-blender until smooth. Check the seasoning and stir in the chopped dill.

- Heat the remaining oil in a large shallow frying pan. Add the prawns and stir around to coat with the oil, then pour on the tomato sauce and ouzo. Cover and simmer for 4-5 minutes or until the prawns have turned pink and the sauce is hot.

- Remove the lid, add the cubes of feta, and fold through the sauce without crumbling the cheese. After 20 seconds or so, spoon the saucy prawns and cheese from the pan into serving bowls. Serve immediately with lemon wedges to garnish.

Tirokafteri

Serves 4–6

350g feta cheese
250g thick Greek yoghurt
1 small Bird's eye chilli, (deseeded
    for less heat)
100ml olive oil
4 tomatoes, diced
A drizzle of extra virgin olive oil

Tirokafteri, which translates as 'hot cheese', is a traditional cheese spread salad which differs from region to region throughout Greece. Also known as 'kopanisti', it is one of our few spicy traditional dishes. Garnished with refreshing chopped tomatoes, this spicy feta cheese dip is good enough just on its own spread onto pitta bread.

- Crumble the feta cheese into a bowl.

- Blitz together the yoghurt and chilli until smooth.

- Mix the blended yoghurt and the oil into the feta.

- Chill in an airtight container until required or for up to 5 days. Spoon into a shallow plate or bowl, top with the diced tomato and a drizzle of extra virgin olive oil.

Top – Tirokafteri
Left – Dolmades
Right – Melitzanosalata
Bottom – Prawns with feta

Top – Taramasalata
Right – Green Pea Fava
Bottom – Falafel

Green Pea Fava

Serves 4–6

350g green split peas
1 small onion, finely chopped
1 stick celery, finely chopped
2 cloves of garlic, finely chopped
   or minced
250ml extra virgin olive oil

FOR THE SALSA:
4 ripe but firm tomatoes, diced
2 red onions, diced
1 small red chilli, deseeded and
   finely chopped
Sea salt and freshly ground
   black pepper

Greek Fava is creamy comfort food: rustic, hearty and nutritious, it is so good on its own but goes particularly well with dark leafy greens and with salty ingredients like anchovies, sardines or feta. This addictive purée also adds a wonderful splash of vibrant green colour topped with salsa as one of a selection of little meze dishes.

- Place the split peas, onion, celery and garlic in a large saucepan. Add 1 litre water and bring to the boil, skimming to remove any sediment as required. Cover and simmer until the peas have softened.

- Leave the peas to cool a little, then blitz or liquidize the peas in a food processor or blender while adding the olive oil. When smooth and creamy, adjust the seasoning to taste.

- Meanwhile, mix the salsa ingredients together. Season well and chill until required.

- Spread the purée out onto a shallow plate and spoon the salsa in the centre with an extra drizzle of olive oil. Eat warm or cold and store any leftovers in an airtight container in the fridge.

Falafel

Serves 6–8
(makes about 25)

100g dried chickpeas
200g dried, split skinless broad
    beans
1 tsp. ground cumin
1 tsp. ground coriander
½ tsp. ground black pepper
¼ tsp. each of ground cinnamon,
    ginger, allspice and nutmeg
1 onion, finely chopped
4 cloves of garlic, chopped
1 large bunch of coriander,
    roughly chopped
1 small bunch of flat-leaf parsley,
    roughly chopped
½ tsp. baking powder
Sea salt, to taste
Sunflower or vegetable oil, to fry

The origin of falafel is unknown and controversial. We Greeks like to think that everything started with us but I have a sneaky feeling falafel originated in Egypt, in Alexandria, possibly eaten by the Copts as a replacement for meat during lent.

Served on a bed of yoghurt and tahini dip, these spicy deep-fried balls or patties are made from ground chickpeas and fava beans. Falafel is a traditional Middle Eastern food usually served with pitta bread. Shapes, sizes and spices vary, but this is our popular version.

- Soak the chickpeas and broad beans in separate bowls of plenty of cold water overnight. Drain and tip on to a clean tea towel to dry.

- Put the beans and half the chickpeas into a food processor and blitz until smooth (be careful not to overload your processor). Add the spices, onion and garlic and blitz again, until well mixed. Now add the remaining chickpeas, herbs and 1 tsp. salt to season. Pulse until well combined, but not a purée – still slightly lumpy with chickpeas.

- Heat a little oil in a small frying pan over a high heat and fry a teaspoon of the mixture to check the seasoning. Adjust if necessary, then stir in the baking powder. Chill the mixture for at least 30 minutes.

- Roll the mixture into small, flattish balls, about 5-6cm across. Pour enough oil into a heavy-based deep-lidded pan to fill to 5cm. Heat the oil to 180°C. A cube of bread dropped into the hot oil will turn golden in 15 seconds at this temperature.

- Fry the falafel in batches and drain on kitchen towel.

- Serve with a spicy yoghurt and tahini dip or Htipiti and toasted flatbreads, a Greek salad.

Taramasalata

Serves 4

5 tbsp. fresh fine white
   breadcrumbs
5 tbsp. lemon juice
150g Tarama paste (cod roe)
600ml Greek olive oil
Kalamata olive, to garnish
A drizzle of extra virgin olive oil

Rich, creamy taramasalata is made every day in our restaurant using only naturally undyed tarama, the salted and cured roe of the cod. This Greek speciality is thickened with breadcrumbs or sometimes ground almonds.

- Weigh the breadcrumbs into a bowl then pour on 250ml water and the lemon juice and let it soak for 15 minutes.

- Transfer to a liquidizer, add the tarama paste and blitz on the highest speed to make a very smooth paste.

- With the motor running on a slower speed, very gradually drizzle in half the oil. Do not add too much as the mixture can split – it is a bit like making mayonnaise. Then steadily but slowly pour in the remainder.

- Chill in an airtight container until required. Spoon onto a shallow plate or bowl, top with a Kalamata olive and a drizzle of extra virgin olive oil.

Melitzanosalata

Serves 4–6 people

3-4 medium aubergines
150ml extra virgin olive oil
2 tbsp. lemon juice
3 plump cloves of garlic
150g finely chopped spring
   onions
3 tbsp finely chopped flat-leaf
   parsley
3 tbsp. finely chopped coriander
1 tsp. sea salt
½ tsp. freshly ground black
   pepper
12 Kalamata olives, to garnish

The aubergine is also known as the 'eggplant' from its smaller, plump ivory-skinned cousin grown in Asia. The Mediterranean aubergine is bigger and bulbous, glossy and deep purple, feeling heavy for its size. With a slightly smoky yet bland flavour, its flesh acts like a sponge soaking up the wonderful flavours and ingredients added in recipes. This meze is no exception!

- Preheat the oven to 180°C (fan 160°C) / Gas 4. Lightly oil a large baking sheet. Cut the aubergines in half lengthways, brush well with a little oil, then place cut-side down on a baking sheet. Cook for 45-50 minutes, turning once halfway through cooking.

- When the flesh is very soft, use a spoon to scoop it out into a bowl, discarding the shells. Using a hand-blender, blitz to a smooth purée, season with salt and pepper and stir in the lemon juice. This should make around 600–700ml purée.

- Meanwhile, blitz together the remaining extra virgin olive oil and garlic and set aside.

- Stir the chopped spring onions and herbs into the aubergine purée then drizzle in enough of the garlicky olive oil to make a creamy dip. Adjust the seasoning to taste.

- Spread onto meze plates, drizzle with olive oil and garnish with a couple of olives per person. It is best served at room temperature.

Htipiti – Spicy Feta Dip

Serves 6–8

2-3 large red peppers
400g feta cheese
150ml Greek olive oil
1-2 tsp. freshly ground pepper
⅓ tsp. dried thyme
1 small Bird's eye chilli, deseeded
   and finely chopped, or dried
   chilli flakes, to taste

A gutsy yet simply made spread or dip, htipiti - also known as kopanisti – is the perfect addition to a Mediterranean meze. The salty bite of feta cheese goes well with the sweet yet smoky roasted peppers with a touch of heat from the chilli.

Garnish with a drizzle of Ladolemono (see page 87) and freshly chopped herbs.

- First chargrill or roast the peppers. Cook in a hot oven for 20–25 minutes or until the skin has charred and blistered and the flesh is soft. Or cook over hot coals on a BBQ grill until the pepper is charred and the flesh is soft. Leave to cool, then peel, discard the seeds and place the flesh in a colander to drain.

- Break the feta into medium-sized pieces into a bowl – do not over-crumble it. Add the olive oil, ground pepper and thyme. Mix to a coarse, lumpy consistency.

- Chop the drained peppers into pieces the size of half a peanut and mix with the chopped chilli.

- Fold the feta and pepper mixes together to make a well-blended spread. Store in the fridge in a sealed container until required. Serve chilled.

Houmous

Serves 4

400g dried or canned
   chickpeas, drained,
   brine reserved
3 tbsp. tahini
Juice of 2 lemons
5 cloves of garlic, crushed
3 tbsp. extra virgin olive oil
A pinch of salt, to taste

TO FINISH:
A drizzle of extra virgin olive oil
Freshly chopped flat-leaf
   parsley
A pinch of paprika

This famous Chickpea and tahini dip is a daily food kept in most Greek fridges alongside milk and cheese. It is so nutritious and versatile added into stews, spread onto bread or eaten alongside kebabs. And rarely is meze eaten without including this garlicky dip.

- If using dried chickpeas, measure into a colander and wash under cold running water. Soak in cold water overnight. Rinse, tip into a large saucepan, cover with water, add salt and bring to a steady boil. Cover then simmer for 1–1¼ hours or until tender. Drain thoroughly, reserving approximately 200ml of the cooking liquor.

- If using canned cooked chickpeas, drain, reserving the brine, rinse under cold running water, drain again and tip into a large bowl, holding back a handful to garnish.

- Mash the chickpeas either by hand for a more rustic dip or use a hand-held blender or food processor for a smoother consistency.

- In another bowl mix together the tahini, lemon juice, some of the reserved chickpea liquor and garlic to a smooth but runny consistency. Mix into the chickpea purée.

- Adjust the consistency and flavour as you like, with either extra lemon juice or chickpea brine. Season to taste with salt.

- Cover and chill until required but at least for several hours for the flavours to develop. Serve garnished with a drizzle of olive oil, chopped parsley and the reserved chickpeas or ground paprika.

Gigandes Plaki

Serves 4–6

450g dried gigandes or butter
    beans
2 tsp. fresh thyme leaves
150ml Greek olive oil
2 bay leaves
1 small onion, finely chopped
1 small carrot, finely chopped
1 small leek, finely sliced
1 stick celery, finely chopped
3–4 cloves of garlic, finely
    chopped or minced
200g passata or chopped
    tomatoes
½ small bunch flat-leaf parsley,
    chopped
A handful of freshly torn basil
    leaves
Sea salt and freshly ground
    black pepper

This butterbean stew is eaten in Greece during fasting time. It is delicious served warm with a selection of other meze dishes and grilled meat or fish. Garnish with extra freshly chopped herbs and a splash of Ladolemono (see page 87). I like it with feta cheese crumbled on top.

- Soak the beans in plenty of water overnight. Drain, put into a saucepan with plenty of cold water and bring to a steady boil, skimming off sediment as it rises to the surface.

- Reduce the heat to a steady simmer, add the onion, carrot, leek, celery and garlic, cover and cook for 1 hour, until the beans are almost tender. Add a little extra water if required.

- Add the passata or chopped tomatoes and cook, uncovered, for a further 20 minutes, stirring frequently. Once the beans are very soft, remove from the heat to cool a little, then stir in the olive oil, parsley and basil. Adjust the seasoning to taste.

Kitchen note: For a short cut substitute the dried beans for 2 x 400g cans of butter beans, rinsed and drained. Fry the finely chopped vegetables first in olive oil before adding the remaining ingredients. Cover and gently simmer for 20 minutes or until tender.

Left – Taramasalata
Right – Gigandes Plaki
Bottom – Tiropitakia

Tiropitakia

Serves 6–8

2 tbsp. olive oil
150g leeks, finely sliced
150g baby spinach leaves
200g feta cheese
2tbsp freshly chopped dill

FOR THE BÉCHAMEL SAUCE:
30g butter
30g plain flour
250ml full-fat milk
½ tsp. ground cinnamon
A pinch of ground nutmeg
Sea salt and freshly ground
   black pepper

FOR THE PASTRIES:
275g pack filo pastry
100ml olive oil
75g plain flour
75g fine semolina
2 eggs, beaten
Oil, for deep frying

Our little cheese pies are cooked daily, such is their popularity and continual demand. Filled with feta cheese, creamy leeks and spinach, these crisp filo triangles are a popular snack in Greece, eaten at any time of the day or as part of a meze.

- Heat the olive oil in a large frying pan, then cook the leeks for 4-5 minutes until soft but not coloured. Stir in the spinach and let it wilt over the heat for 1-2 minutes. Season well with black pepper, then transfer to a colander set over a bowl to thoroughly drain off any liquid.

- Make the béchamel sauce: melt the butter over a medium heat in a small saucepan. Blend in the flour and continue to cook, stirring for 30 seconds or so to lightly brown the flour to a paste. Now gradually blend in the milk, a little at a time, and simmer, stirring, to form a smooth, creamy sauce. Season with the cinnamon, a good pinch of nutmeg and salt and pepper, to taste.

- Tip the well-drained leek mixture into a bowl, crumble in the feta and add the dill. Now fold in enough béchamel sauce to bind everything together to make the filling for the pastries.

- Remove the filo pastry from its pack – do not unroll it, but cut into equal thirds. Take one third and unroll to make the first batch of Tiropitakia. Cover the filo you are not using with damp kitchen towel to keep moist.

- Lightly brush the first strip of pastry with oil. Take 1 tsp. of the cheese mix and place it on the bottom corner of the filo, then fold the filo over to make a triangle. Continue to fold up and when 7cm from the end of the strip, brush the filo with oil to then fold and seal the completed triangle. Place on a tray lined with baking parchment. Repeat until the filo and mix is finished.

- Blend the flour and semolina together in one shallow plate and beat the eggs in a second shallow plate. Now dip each triangle into the egg, shake off excess and lightly dust with the flour mix. Transfer to a tray lined with baking parchment and chill for 1 hour or until required.

- Deep fry at 170°C in bàtches for 5 minutes or until golden brown. Drain onto absorbent kitchen towel and serve warm. Alternatively glaze the little pies with beaten egg wash, arrange on a baking sheet and cook in a preheated oven at 200F / 180'F fan / gas 6 for 30 minutes or until golden brown and crisp.

Tzatziki

Serves 4

4 large cloves of garlic, grated or minced
1 tbsp. olive oil, plus extra for dressing
1 large firm cucumber
1 tbsp. lemon juice or white wine vinegar
500g strained natural yoghurt
A handful of dried Greek mint or 3 tbsp. freshly chopped mint or dill
Salt, to taste
Fresh mint sprigs and an olive, to garnish

Cool and refreshingly tangy, this creamy yoghurt and cucumber dip is well known around the world. We all have our own variation and preference, sometimes stronger on sweet mint other times heavy on garlic. Always served chilled, it is great with molten halloumi, kebabs, grilled meats and fish, as a dip, and used as a spread or dressing.

- Crush the garlic into the oil with a pinch of salt and leave to infuse.

- Coarsely grate the cucumber into a colander in the sink. Salt lightly, toss and leave to drain for 30 minutes.

- Stir the garlicky oil and lemon juice or vinegar into the yoghurt. Squeeze out the cucumber very well, then stir this in, too. Allow to sit for a couple of hours.

- Just before serving, season to taste, adding more oil or vinegar if necessary, then rub the dried mint between your fingers to crumble into the yoghurt. Alternatively, add some finely chopped dill or mint (discarding the tough stems) and stir into the tzatziki. Garnish with an olive.

Kitchen note: Dried Greek mint is used a lot in place of fresh mint for crumbling into dishes as it has a stronger, sweet taste.

Top Right – Tzatziki
Bottom Right – Revithia
Centre Left – Dukkah

Revithia – Chickpeas

Serves 4–6

500g dried chickpeas
1 onion, finely chopped
1 carrot, finely chopped
1 small leek, finely sliced
1 stick celery, finely chopped
3–4 cloves of garlic, finely
    chopped or minced
Juice of 3 large lemons
    (approx. 100ml)
Zest of 1 lemon
200ml olive oil
2 tbsp. finely shredded sage
    leaves
Sea salt and freshly ground
    black pepper

Revithia was traditionally made using chickpeas baked with onions in olive oil and flavoured with bay leaf and rosemary. The pot would be taken to the local bakery to be cooked overnight in their oven. The Real Greek recipe stirs in sage and plenty of fresh lemon...and is just as delicious!

- Soak the chickpeas in plenty of water overnight. Drain, put in a saucepan with 1 litre of cold water and add the onion, carrot, leek, celery and garlic. Bring to the boil, skimming away any sediment. Reduce the heat to a simmer, cover and cook until the chickpeas are tender, adding a little extra water if required.

- In a large bowl, mix together the lemon juice, zest, olive oil, sage and a little black pepper.

- Drain the chickpeas thoroughly and stir into the dressing. Season with salt to taste and serve warm.

Kitchen note: For a short cut substitute the dried chickpeas for 2 x 400g cans of chickpeas, rinsed and drained. Fry the finely chopped vegetables first in olive oil before adding the chickpeas. Then mix into the dressing.

Dukkah with Greek Flatbread

Serves 4

8 flatbreads
100g dukkah
100ml extra virgin olive oil
3 tbsp. garlic-infused oil

FOR THE ANATOLIAN SPICE:

3 tbsp. cumin seeds
1 tbsp. caraway seeds
2 tsp. coriander seeds
2 tsp. yellow mustard seeds
1 tsp. fennel seeds
1 tsp. garlic granules
1 tsp. paprika
5cm strip of lemon peel,
    pith removed

FOR THE DUKKAH:

2 tsp. Anatolian spice
300g hazelnuts
2 tbsp. sesame seeds
1 tbsp. (approx 10g) Shichimi
    (Japanese 7-spice chilli
    powder)
1 tsp. onion powder
1 tsp. garlic powder
1 tsp. salt

Dukkah is an Egyptian spicy mix of nuts – commonly hazelnuts – and seeds, but each region and indeed Middle Eastern country have their own blend or version. The name 'dukkah' means 'to crush' or 'to pound' in its native Egyptian, and this aromatic blend is delicious spread onto flatbreads or used as a dip after dipping bread into olive oil first..

Enjoy our version.

- First make the Anatolian spice blend. This can be made ahead as it keeps well, stored in a lidded jam jar in a cool dark place. Spread all the ingredients out onto a small baking tray and roast in a preheated oven at 170°C (fan 150°C) / Gas 4 for 1 hour or until very fragrant and looking toasty. Using a coffee grinder or hand-held blender, grind to a very fine powder.

- For the dukkah, again spread all the ingredients out onto a small baking tray and roast in a preheated oven at 170°C (fan 150°C) / Gas 4 for 1 hour or until looking toasty. Using a coffee grinder or hand-held blender, grind to a coarse, sandy texture.

- To serve, brush a little garlic oil onto the flatbreads. Place the flatbreads into a frying pan, in batches, or under a grill and cook on a medium heat until golden brown on both sides.

- Slice the flatbreads into triangular pieces (n.b. as per the photo) for dipping.

- Arrange 2 small dipping bowls on a large board or plate. Fill one with olive oil and the other with dukkah mix. Place the bread triangles alongside and serve.

Grilled Mezes

Grilled Halloumi

Serves 4

500g halloumi
    (see page 97)
Ladolemono (see page 87)
Freshly chopped flat-leaf
    parsley, to garnish
pickled onion and cabbage
    garnish

Halloumi is a Cypriot semi-hard, unripened brined cheese made from a mixture of goat's and sheep's milk. With its high melting point, it is ideal for frying or grilling –it softens rather than melts and is sometimes known as the 'squeaky' cheese!

- Lightly oil a heavy-based frying pan or griddle pan and set over a medium-high heat.

- Cut the halloumi into 1cm slices and place in the hot pan. Cook for 2 minutes on each side or until the cheese has softened with a nice golden-brown crust.

- Arrange 3-4 slices per person fanned out onto individual plates. Drizzle with a little ladolemono and garnish with freshly chopped parsley. Serve with a spoonful of onion and cabbage garnish.

Kitchen note: Our pickled onion and cabbage garnish is easy to make and so good with halloumi and grilled meats. Make at least 24 hours ahead for the best flavour and crunch.

Halloumi and Vegetable Skewers

Serves 4

600g halloumi
1 red pepper, deseeded and cut
    into 2cm pieces
2 courgette, cut into 1cm slices
1 tbsp. finely chopped mint
150g Greek yoghurt
Pickled onion and cabbage
    garnish (see page 97)
Ladolemono (see page 87)
Olive oil, to brush

Serve these skewers with a minty flavoured yoghurt or cooling tzatziki.

- Cut the halloumi into 3cm chunks. Thread onto skewers alternating with the red pepper and courgette. Repeat to make 4 skewers.

- Stir the mint into the yoghurt and chill until required.

- Preheat the grill or a large frying pan and brush with a little oil. Cook the skewers for 8–10 minutes, turning every 2–3 minutes or until the cheese has softened and formed a golden-brown crust.

- Serve the skewers drizzled with a little ladolemono and a spoonful of onion and cabbage garnish.

Grilled Aubergine with Tomato and Garlic Sauce

Serves 4–6

1kg aubergine (approx. 4 large)
50g garlic paste or 6 cloves
   of garlic, minced
olive oil for frying

FOR THE TOMATO SAUCE:
500g passata
200g red onion
100g sofrito
1 tsp. finely chopped rosemary
1 tsp. finely chopped sage leaves
1 tbsp. freshly chopped flat-leaf
   parsley
1 bay leaf
2 sprigs of fresh thyme
100ml extra virgin olive oil
1 tbsp. ground paprika
Sea salt and freshly ground
   black pepper

Topped with a tangy pasta style sauce, these succulent aubergine rings go well with bread and olives on the side.

- Make the tomato sauce: Using a food processor or hand-held blender, blitz together the passata, onion, sofrito, rosemary, sage, bay leaf parsley and thyme. Pour into a pan and add 200ml water. Cover and simmer for 45 minutes until thickened. Season to taste. Stir in the extra virgin olive oil and the paprika and plenty of black pepper. Remove from the heat.

- Slice the aubergine into 2.5cm rings. Place in a bowl with salt, pepper and the garlic paste and move the rings around to cook. Leave for 10 minutes.

- Place a griddle pan or large frying pan over a medium-heat with a little oil. Grill the aubergine rings, in batches, for 3-4 minutes on each side or until softened in the middle.

- Build stacks of aubergine slices onto 4 individual plates, then spoon the tomato sauce down one side of the aubergine. Garnish with freshly chopped green herbs of your choice and serve.

Grilled Kalamari (or Grilled Squid)

Serves 4–6

750g fresh squid, cleaned
100ml olive oil

FOR THE SQUID MARINADE:
300ml olive oil
100g Greek runny honey,
    at a warm room temperature
2 tbsp. 50g (approx.) ground
    paprika
3 cloves of garlic
2 tsp. Greek mountain
    oregano

TO SERVE:
Ribbons of carrot and cucumber
2 tsp. ladolemono (see page 87)
2 tsp. freshly chopped green
    herbs
2 lemons, cut into wedges
Sea salt and freshly ground
    black pepper

Kalamari is a Greek Island staple, usually served simply with just a few spices..

We use the freshest squid, and grill it until tender.

- Make the marinade:. Blitz together all the ingredients in a blender or liquidizer until smooth. Season to taste and set aside.

- Prepare the squid. Using a sharp knife, cut the body piece (mantle) into two down the middle then score a criss-cross pattern on the outer side of the flesh. Cut the flesh into 3cm square pieces.

- Score the wings of the squid and again cut into 3cm square pieces.

- Cut the long tentacles in half, and trim the head and arms into smaller pieces.

- Place the marinade and squid pieces in a large bowl, mixing well to coat.

- Place a griddle or frying pan over a medium-high heat. Drain the marinated squid and cook in the hot pan for 3 minutes on each side.

- Divide onto individual serving plates and garnish with ribbons of carrot and cucumber (see below), ladolemono, freshly chopped herbs and lemon wedges for squeezing. Season to taste.

Kitchen note: Make a simple garnish of carrot and cucumber using a potato peeler to cut them into ribbons.

Grilled Octopus

Serves 4–6

1.5kg fresh octopus, cleaned
100ml olive oil
ribbons of carrot and cucumber
    (see page 51) and lemon
wedges, to serve

FOR THE DRESSING:
Juice of 3 lemons (approx, 90ml)
75g Dijon mustard
2 cloves of garlic
1 heaped tsp. of Greek mountain
    oregano
350ml extra virgin olive oil
Sea salt and freshly ground
    black pepper
A pinch of ground paprika
1 tbsp. freshly chopped green
    herbs

The classic Greek dish of freshly caught chargrilled octopus is cooked with olive oil, garlic and our most-used culinary herb wild Greek oregano – arguably the best oregano in the world!. This wild herb grows abundantly on Mount Taygetos, the highest mountain in Lakonía, Greece and has a robust, pungent flavour, which is characteristic in Mediterranean cooking. Meaning 'Joy of the mountain', the Greek name 'origanon' refers to oros, meaning 'mountain', and the verb ganousthai, meaning 'delight in'. It is worth bringing some dried wild oregano back with you from your holiday travels to Greece.

- Preheat the oven to 150°C (fan 130°C) / Gas 2.

- Place the cleaned octopus in a large roasting tray and drizzle with olive oil. Cook for 2–2½ hours or until tender. Remove and cut into portions.

- To make the dressing, blitz together all the ingredients except the olive oil in a blender or liquidizer. Gradually trickle in the olive oil to form an emulsion. Season to taste and set aside.

- Preheat a grill or griddle and cook the portions for 2-3 minutes until lightly charred. Cut into 1cm slices.

- Serve on individual plates garnished with ribbons of carrot and cucumber, lemon wedges and a generous drizzle of the dressing.

Chicken Gyros

Serves 4–6

900g boneless chicken thighs,
   skin on
1 red onion, halved and finely
   sliced
1 tomato, halved and sliced
1 tsp. ground paprika

FOR THE GYROS MARINADE:
5 tbsp. olive oil
5 tbsp. lemon juice
100g ground cumin
50g sea salt
3 tbsp. ground sweet paprika
3 tbsp. garlic purée
2 tbsp. finely chopped flat-leaf
   parsley
2 tsp. ground cinnamon

The most important step in making traditional chicken gyros is the marinade. Tender chicken thighs should be steeped in a salt-based marinade (almi), along with Mediterranean herbs and earthy spices, then roasted or grilled until crunchy and irresistible. And if that is not enough, most Greeks enjoy their traditional Greek chicken gyro with chips... and a creamy yoghurt dip. Wrapped in warm pitta is another favourite way.

- In a large bowl, mix together the ingredients for the marinade. Add the chicken, rubbing the thighs well, then marinate for no more than 30 minutes.

- Drain the chicken from the marinade and wipe with absorbent kitchen towel. To achieve the desired crunchiness, fry the gyro in a very hot large non-stick pan for 5-6 minutes on each side, without stirring, until nicely coloured. Open one piece up to see if it is cooked (there should be no pink in the middle).

- Alternatively tightly pack into a shallow dish and roast in a preheated oven 180°C (fan 160°C) / Gas 4 for 1 hour 20 minutes or until very crispy and well coloured with no pink juices running when pierced.

- To serve, slice into 1cm pieces or dice and pile onto warm flatbreads on individual serving plates. Top with the finely sliced onion and a sprinkling of paprika.

Chicken Skewers

Serves 4–6

6 chicken breasts, boneless and
    skinless, cut into 3cm chunks
1 small red pepper, deseeded
1 small yellow pepper, deseeded
1 red onion

FOR THE MARINADE:
2 tbsp. olive oil
2 tbsp. lemon juice
1 tsp. freshly chopped rosemary
1 tsp. freshly chopped thyme
    leaves
1 tsp. ground paprika
Sea salt and freshly ground
    black pepper

TO SERVE:
300g lemon mayonnaise (see
    page 87)
75g onion and cabbage garnish
    (see page 97)
2 tsp. ladolemono (see page 87)

Skewers of tender marinated chicken grilled with peppers
and onions, with irresistible lemon mayo on the side
for dipping! For a healthier option you can always opt
for tzatziki (see page 57) instead. The great thing with
meze is that nothing is set in stone and dishes are so
interchangeable – a relaxed and healthy way of eating.

- In a large bowl, mix together the ingredients for the
  marinade. Season with salt and pepper. Add the chicken
  chunks, coating them well, then marinate for at least 1 hour,
  but preferably longer. (Ideally overnight in the fridge).

- Cut the peppers (if following the advice above) into 2cm
  pieces. Quarter the onion and cut the leaves into 2cm
  pieces.

- Soak 6 wooden skewers to prevent them from charring.
  When ready to cook, thread the chicken, peppers and
  onion alternately onto the skewers. Season with salt and
  pepper.

- Cook under a medium-hot grill or in a griddle pan for 8-10
  minutes, turning every couple of minutes and basting with
  any remaining marinade.

- Cut each skewer in half and arrange crossways on
  individual serving plates. Serve with a small pot of lemon
  mayonnaise, a drizzling of ladolemono and a spoonful of
  onion and cabbage garnish.

Dukkah Chicken Wings

Serves 4–6

1.5kg chicken wings
100g dukkah seasoning
  (see page 41)
200ml light olive oil
200g chilli relish (see page 93)
2 spring onions, finely chopped
1 tbsp. freshly chopped dill or
  flat-leaf parsley
Sea salt and freshly ground
  black pepper

Our spicy house blend of dukkah is used to dust tasty chicken wings before grilling, and if that is not enough we serve them with our lively chilli relish. They are delicious with warmed pitta bread, cooling tzaziki (see page 37) and enjoyed as part of a meze.

- Simmer the chicken wings in a large pan of lightly salted water for 20 minutes or until cooked. Carefully pour into a large colander and drain thoroughly.

- Whilst the chicken is still warm, tip into a large bowl, add the Dukkah and oil. Season with salt and pepper and mix together thoroughly to coat.

- Arrange on a griddle pan or under a medium-hot grill and cook for 4 minutes on each side until well coloured and cooked through.

- Serve on a large plate sprinkled with a little more dukkah, with the chopped spring onion, herbs and chilli relish on the side.

Grilled Lamb Cutlets

Sweet and succulent, lamb cutlets need little else than a hot flame and a keen eye.

- Remove from the refrigerator and allow the cutlets to come to room temperature, which will take about 15 minutes.

- Heat a griddle or grill pan over a high heat until almost smoking, add the cutlets and sear for about 2 minutes.

- Turn the chops over and cook for another 3 minutes for medium-rare and 3½ minutes for medium.

Recipe for Lentils found on page 77 and served with minted yoghurt.

Lamb Kefte

Serves 4–6

FOR THE LAMB KEFTE MIX:
1kg lean minced lamb
5g Anatolian spice (see page 41)
75g fresh white breadcrumbs
1 egg, beaten
100g spring onions, finely
   chopped
3 tbsp. freshly chopped mint
3 tbsp. freshly chopped flat-leaf
   parsley
Sea salt and freshly ground
   black pepper
olive oil for brushing

TO SERVE:
200g Greek yoghurt
1 tbsp. finely chopped mint
4 tbsp. Pickled onion and
   cabbage garnish
   (see page 97)
8 tsp. ladolemono (see page 87)

Lean lamb, minced and marinated with our special blend of Anatolian spices, can be formed into patties or meatballs, served burger-style or skewered...

- Put the minced lamb, spice, breadcrumbs and egg into a large bowl and knead together well, as if making bread. Mix in the spring onions, mint and parsley. Season well with salt and plenty of pepper.

- Take equal size amounts of the mix 175g (approx/each) and mould into oval patties.

- Place in an oiled griddle pan or under a medium-hot grill and cook for approximately 10 minutes, turning frequently.

- Serve the lamb kefte with minty yoghurt, made simply by combining the yoghurt and mint, with an onion and cabbage garnish on the side. Finish with a drizzle of ladolemono.

Lamb Meatballs

Serves 4–6

FOR THE LAMB KEFTE MIX:

1kg lean minced lamb

5g Anatolian spice (see page 41)

75g fresh white breadcrumbs

1 egg, beaten

100g spring onions, finely
   chopped

3 tbsp. freshly chopped mint

3 tbsp. freshly chopped flat-leaf
   parsley

Sea salt and freshly ground
   black pepper

TO SERVE:

300g Greek yoghurt

300g hot tomato sauce

200g red onions, finely sliced

1 tsp. ground paprika

Our handmade patties or meatballs topped with yoghurt
and a robust tomato sauce is a meal in itself but if you can
bear to share in a meze, they are really good with a Greek
salad and houmous (see page 31).

- Put the minced lamb, spice, breadcrumbs and egg into a
  large bowl and knead together well, as if making bread.
  Mix in the spring onions, mint and parsley. Season well with
  salt and plenty of pepper.

- Take equal-sized amounts of the mix 50g (approx./each)
  and mould each into meatballs.

- Place in an oiled griddle pan or under a medium-hot grill
  and cook for approximately 8 minutes, turning frequently.

- Place 3 meatballs each on 4 serving plates. Spoon some
  yoghurt over the top of the meatballs, then place another
  meatball on and ladle over some hot tomato sauce, to
  cover and melt into the yoghurt.

- Top with the onion slices and a generous sprinkling of
  paprika before serving.

Lamb Skewers

Serves 4–6

1.5kg leg of lamb steak, cut into
   2cm cubes
1 red onion, quartered
1 small red pepper, deseeded

FOR THE MARINADE:
75g Greek yoghurt
2 tsp. freshly chopped rosemary
1 tsp. freshly chopped thyme
2 tsp. paprika
½ tsp. ground cumin
Sea salt, to taste

TO SERVE:
175g lemon mayonnaise
   (see page 87)
4–6 tbsp. pickled onion and
   cabbage garnish (see page
   97)
Greek salad (see page 81)
4 tsp. ladolemono (see page 87)

- Mix together the marinade ingredients, seasoning well with salt. Add the lamb and mix well to coat. Cover and leave to marinade in a cool place for at least 1 hour or overnight in the fridge.

- Separate the onion leaves and cut into 3cm pieces. Cut the pepper into 2cm pieces.

- Starting and ending with the lamb, thread the meat, onion and pepper onto 4–6 skewers.

- Place under a medium-hot grill and cook for approximately 8–10 minutes, turning every 2–3 minutes.

- Serve the skewers with lemon mayonnaise, the onion and cabbage garnish and a drizzle of ladolemono.

Salt Cod

Serves 4 - 6

1kg cod, boneless, cut into 200g
    portions
300g white sugar
600g salt
Vegetable oil, for deep frying

FOR THE BEER BATTER:
450g plain flour
750ml beer
½ tsp. ground paprika
A generous pinch of Sea salt

Plan ahead and salt your own cod for this delicious beer battered fish dish. Serve with lemon wedges, our lemon mayonnaise and a sprinkling of Green Herb Garnish...not forgetting a side of chips...

- To salt the cod, mix the sugar and salt together then sprinkle enough to cover the base of a lidded container. Arrange a single layer of fillets skin side up, cover with more sugar and salt and continue layering until all the cod is covered.

- Cover and refrigerate for 48 hours. Remove and soak the cured cod in 4 litres of water in a cool place for 8 hours. Refresh the water and leave again for another 8 hours by which time the salted cod can be well drained and is ready to use.

- To make the batter, place all the ingredients in a large bowl and whisk until smooth.

- Heat some oil in an electric fryer to 170°C. Cut the salt cod into 3cm x ½ cm strips and pierce onto a skewer. Dip in the batter then, ensuring the basket is lowered into the hot oil first, add the salt cod and fry for 4 minutes or until the batter is golden and crisp. Drain in the basket for 30 seconds.

- Repeat until all the cod is cooked.

- Stack 4 crispy strips of fish onto each meze plate and serve immediately.

Slow Roasted Pork Belly

Serves 4

800g piece of pork belly
2 red onions, halved and finely
    sliced
2 tsp. ground paprika

FOR THE MARINADE:
100ml fresh orange juice
3 heaped tbsp. Dijon mustard
2 tbsp. runny Greek honey
2 tsp. dried marjoram
2 tsp. fennel seeds
2 tsp. ground sweet paprika
2 tbsp. sea salt
3 garlic cloves (50g)
2 tbsp. finely chopped flat-leaf
    parsley
1 tsp. ground cinnamon

Slow roasted pork belly prepared the way we do our pork gyros in Greece – in a sweet orange and honey marinade. Pile onto warmed flatbread or into crisp lettuce leaves with your favourite dip spooned alongside.

- Using a hand-held blender or food processor, blitz the marinade ingredients to a smooth paste.

- Rub the marinade onto both sides of the pork belly. Roll the meat up and secure with butchers string.

- Roast in a preheated oven 180°C (fan 160°C) / Gas 4 for 1 hour 30 minutes or until very tender.

- To serve, carve into 2.5 cm slices then roughly chop into 1cm dice and pile onto individual serving plates. Top with the finely sliced onion and a sprinkling of paprika.

Souvlaki

All our Greek souvlakis are served the same, Athenian street style.

- Take a fresh flatbread and dollop a healthy serving of tzatziki in the middle, spread around the flatbread, then place your choice of filling – strips of cooked chicken, pork or lamb, or falafel or slices of halloumi.

- Top with sliced ripe tomatoes, lots of red onion slivers and finish with a sprinkling of freshly chopped parsley and a dusting of paprika.

- Fold in the ends of the flatbread, then roll your souvlaki up and 'Opa'... you are ready to go!

All the recipes for fillings are available in this chapter, including Grilled Halloumi (p.45), Chicken Skewers (p.57), Lamb Kefte (p.63) and Pork Belly (p.71).

Salads and Sides

Beetroot, Lentil and Feta Salad

Serves 4–6

100g sofrito mix
450g green lentils
125ml extra virgin olive oil
3 tbsp. lemon juice
250g cooked beetroot, cut into
    ½ cm cubes
200g feta cheese, cut into ½ cm
    cubes
1 tbsp. ladolemono (see page 87)
Freshly torn flat-leaf parsley,
    to garnish
Sea salt and freshly ground
    black pepper, to taste

Many supermarkets now sell sofrito – a packet of colourful chopped onion, carrot, celery, leeks or onion and garlic – so handy for adding to soups and pulses for flavour when cooking. Or you can chop up your own!

Ladolemono (which means oil and lemon) appears in many Greek recipes. With its equal lemon juice to oil ratio, it is a lively, fresh and sharp lemon dressing often used at the table to splash over grilled meat, fish, salads and beans. Make a handy jar of it to store in the fridge.

- Using a hand-held blender, blitz the sofrito with 2 tbsp. of the olive oil to a fine mince.

- Place the lentils and minced sofrito in a saucepan with 700ml lightly salted water. Bring to the boil, cover and simmer until the lentils are just tender. Drain thoroughly and tip into a bowl.

- Stir in the olive oil and lemon juice. Season to taste with salt and pepper. Leave to cool slightly.

- Spread the lentils onto a shallow serving plate then scatter on the beetroot and feta.

- Drizzle with ladolemono and scatter with parsley. Serve at room temperature as part of a meze.

Couscous Salad

Serves 6–8

400g couscous
100g dried cranberries
2 red onions, finely chopped
10 spring onions, trimmed and
   finely sliced
8 preserved lemons, finely sliced
1 Bird's eye chilli, finely chopped
Juice of 3 large lemons
5 tbsp. extra virgin olive oil
5 tbsp. freshly chopped mint
   leaves plus extra, to garnish
5 tbsp. freshly chopped
   coriander
5 tbsp. freshly chopped flat-leaf
   parsley
Tomato and onion salsa, to serve
   (optional)

This is a healthy and vibrant salad developed by Tonia and a popular side dish at The Real Greek. Couscous soaks up flavours and this one has plenty going for it. It's delicious with grilled lamb cutlets (see page 61) and lamb kefte (see page 63) with tzatziki (see page 37) for dolloping.

- Prepare the couscous according to the packet instructions. Tip into a large bowl and stir in the dried cranberries. Leave to cool.

- Stir in all the remaining ingredients and combine well. Cover and chill for 1 hour to let the flavours develop.

- Serve at room temperature, topped, if liked, with tomato and onion salsa.

Kitchen note: A fresh tomato salsa is a great garnish for this couscous salad. Finely dice and mix together 4 tomatoes, 1 red onion and a Bird's eye chilli (deseeded for a milder heat). Season and spoon on the centre of the couscous, topped with fresh mint leaves.

Greek Salad

Serves 6

2kg firm, ripe tomatoes,
    quartered
1 large cucumber, cut into 2.5cm
    batons
2 red onions, sliced
1 green pepper, deseeded and
    sliced
125ml extra virgin olive oil
2 tbsp. red wine vinegar
300g feta cheese
1 tsp. dried oregano
100g Kalamata olives
Salt, to taste

Classic and rustic, our Horiatiki Salata, also known as a village salad, is brought to the table at every mealtime in Greece or in just about any Greek restaurant anywhere in the world. The secret to making this chunky, colourful but simple salad lies in the freshest ingredients and finest Greek olive oil. This is The Real Greek salad...

- Place the tomatoes, cucumber, onions and green pepper in a large serving bowl.

- Whisk together the olive oil and red wine vinegar. Season with salt. Drizzle as much or as little as you like over the chopped salad, tossing through to coat.

- Cut the feta into 4 slabs.

- To serve, sprinkle half the oregano over the salad, then top with the feta, sprinkle on the remaining oregano and finish with the olives.

- Serve with a fork and spoon, which is traditionally used to break up the feta and toss through the salad before sharing around.

Saffron Rice with Honey Saffron Dressing

Serves 6–8

FOR THE DRESSING:
1 tbsp. lemon juice
A pinch of saffron threads
3 tbsp. clear honey
6 tbsp. olive oil
Sea salt and freshly ground
    black pepper

400g easy-cook long-grain rice
1 tsp. dried oregano
A large pinch of saffron threads
25g ghee
A pinch of salt
Fresh chopped herbs, to garnish

A pinch of saffron in a honey dressing is delicious drizzled over this fragrant rice but equally good to glaze grilled fish and chicken.

- To make the dressing, gently heat the lemon juice and saffron in a very small saucepan for about 30 seconds, until you can see the saffron dissolve and colour the liquid. Leave to cool, then whisk in the honey and olive oil and season.

- Put the rice, oregano and saffron in a large pan with 700ml water. Add a pinch of salt, then bring to the boil, reduce the heat, and simmer for 10 minutes or until the rice is tender. Drain thoroughly.

- Mix the ghee into the hot rice and tip into a serving dish. Drizzle on as little or as much dressing as you like. Garnish with fresh chopped herbs.

Kitchen note: If you do not have ghee, substitute it with a little olive oil or melted clarified butter.

Garnishes and Sauces

Ladolemono

Makes 150ml

125ml extra virgin olive oil
Juice of ½ lemon (approx. 25ml)
Healthy pinch of salt

A little goes a long way when you drizzle this citrusy dressing over simply cooked foods. A blend of olive oil and lemon, this is a classic accompaniment to grilled fish, chicken and vegetables and is also a great salad dressing.

- Simply add the oil, strained lemon juice and salt into a clean dressing bottle or jar and shake well before using. Store in a cool, dark place.

Lemon Mayonnaise

Makes approx. 500ml

4 medium egg yolks
1 tbsp. white wine vinegar
30g preserved lemons
2 tsp. Dijon mustard
425ml light olive oil
Sea salt and white pepper, to taste

Cover tightly and keep well chilled for up to 1 week. It's delicious with grilled chicken and fish.

- Using a food processor or hand-held blender, blitz together the egg yolks, vinegar, preserved lemon and mustard.

- With the machine running on a low speed, gradually drizzle in the oil until the mayonnaise emulsifies and thickens to a smooth consistency. Season with salt and white pepper.

- Cover and chill until required but at least for several hours for the flavours to develop.

Kitchen note: If you do not have preserved lemons, use the finely grated zest of 1 lemon or to taste.

Tomato Sauce

Serves 4-6

500g tomato passata
200g red onion
100g sofrito (available from all
good supermarkets)
1 tsp finely chopped rosemary
1 tsp finely chopped sage leaves
1 tbsp. freshly chopped parsley
or sage
2 sprigs of fresh thyme
1 bay leaf
100ml extra virgin olive oil
1 tbsp. ground paprika
Sea salt and freshly ground
black pepper

**Our wonderful Greek pasta sauce lends itself to so many
Mediterranean recipes**

- Using a food processor or hand blender, blitz together the
tomato passata, onion, sofrito, rosemary, sage, bay leaf and
thyme. Pour into a pan and add 200ml water.

- Cover and simmer for 45 minutes until thickened. Season to
taste.

- Stir in the extra virgin olive oil and the paprika and plenty of
black pepper. The sauce is now ready to use.

Chilli Relish

Makes 1kg

125g chipotle chillies
100ml white wine vinegar
1 onion, quartered
50g fresh coriander with stems
200g granulated sugar
1 tbsp. black treacle
200g tomato purée

This relish is not too hot, but has a cheeky little kick to liven up grilled meats and vegetables, and it's just great for scooping onto flatbreads, or stirring into creamy feta cheese or cooling yoghurt dips.

• Soak the chillies in the vinegar together with the onion and half the coriander for 20–30 minutes. Then, using a food processor or hand-held blender, blitz together to make a smooth paste.

• Put the sugar and 350ml water in a large pan and stir in the treacle. Cover and bring to a steady simmer. Stir in the tomato purée and salt. Boil steadily for 10 minutes.

• Stir in the chilli paste and simmer over a medium heat for a further 20 minutes or until glossy and thickened.

• Finely chop the remaining coriander leaves and stalks and stir into the relish. Carefully spoon into clean sterile jars, cool, then cover and store in a dark place. Once opened, keep in the fridge.

Kitchen note: To sterilize jars, wash in hot, soapy water, rinse, then dry in an oven pre-heated to 150°C (fan 130°C) / Gas 2. Or run through a dishwasher on its hottest setting.

Green Herb Garnish

Serves 4–6

50g flat-leaf parsley, leaves only
25g dill
50g spring onions, finely
   chopped

This simple garnish adds a fresh, vibrant finish to meze dishes and while you can use your favourite herbs, this combination is perfect.

- Finely chop the parsley and dill and mix in with the spring onions. Store in a lidded container in the fridge until required.

Pickled Onion and Cabbage Garnish

Serves 4–8

350g white cabbage
350g red onion
700ml white wine vinegar
150g granulated sugar
2 tsp. sea salt
1 tsp. freshly chopped thyme
    leaves

Quick pickling is an easy way to turn vegetables into crisp-textured slaws or ribbons to pile high alongside meze. With its refreshing crunch and sweet and sour flavour, this garnish is quite addictive!

- Using a mandolin or mini food processor, finely shred the cabbage and onion. Set aside.

- In a large glass bowl, mix together the vinegar, sugar, salt and thyme leaves with 200ml cold water. Add the shredded cabbage and onion to the liquid, submerging it completely. Use a saucer to weigh the ingredients down if required.

- Cover and refrigerate overnight. After 24 hours, the garnish is ready to use.

Kitchen note: For a colourful cucumber and carrot garnish, make using the same method above but, using a potato peeler, cut long ribbons of carrot and cucumber into the vinegar solution. Fennel, celery, radish and kale work well too.

Chef's Specials

Oven Mixed Vegetables

Kostas' Mum's recipe

Serves 4–6

1kg waxy potatoes, cut into
    chunks
1kg aubergines, thickly sliced
700g courgettes, thickly sliced
4 green peppers, deseeded and
    thickly sliced
4 red peppers, deseeded and
    thickly sliced
250ml Greek extra virgin olive oil
400g can chopped tomatoes
1 tbsp. dried oregano
2 large red onions
3–4 cloves of garlic
200g feta cheese, crumbled
    (optional)
Sea salt and freshly ground
    black pepper

This recipe comes from the kitchen of our Soho manager,
Kostas' mum. It's a real family favourite.

Greek cuisine is full of wonderful vegan and vegetarian
dishes, and this is a great example of that.

- Preheat the oven to 200°C (fan 180°F) / Gas 6. Boil the
  potatoes for 10 minutes, then drain thoroughly and
  spread into a large baking tray.

- Mix the aubergines, courgettes and peppers in with the
  potatoes and pour on the olive oil and chopped tomatoes.
  Season well with sea salt and freshly ground black pepper.
  Sprinkle in the oregano and pour on 150ml water.

- Use a blender to purée the onions and garlic, then pour this
  mixture over the vegetables. Bake for 35-40 minutes or until
  the vegetables are tender and well coloured. If the surface
  is browning too quickly, cover with a sheet of foil.

- If adding the feta, 5 minutes before the end of cooking
  time, crumble the cheese over the vegetables and return
  to the oven to soften.

Stella Stathopoulou

Stuffed Aubergines

'Melitzanes papoutsakia' or aubergine 'slippers' is a dish which gets its name from the resemblance of its shape to little shoes.

Serves 6

5 medium aubergines
Olive oil, for cooking

FOR THE MEAT FILLING:
250g minced beef
1 large onion, finely chopped
1 tsp. dried wild (or Mountain) oregano
¼ tsp. ground cinnamon
1 clove of garlic, finely chopped
125ml Greek red wine
400g can chopped tomatoes
A pinch of sugar
25g kefalotyri cheese, grated (optional)
Sea salt and freshly ground black pepper, to taste

FOR THE BÉCHAMEL SAUCE:
25g butter
25g plain flour
250ml full-fat milk
2 egg yolks
50g Kefalotyri cheese (or a hard Cheddar–style cheese), grated
A pinch of ground nutmeg

- Cut the aubergines in half lengthwise. Using a small sharp tipped knife, score the flesh in a crisscross manner. Season the cut sides generously with salt. Set aside for 20 minutes to release the bitter flavours. Rinse and pat dry with absorbent kitchen towel.

- Preheat the oven to 200°C (fan 180°C) / Gas 6.

- Season the aubergines cut side up with salt and pepper and a drizzle of olive oil.

- Place cut side down onto a baking tray and cook for 30 minutes or until tender.

- Meanwhile prepare the meat sauce. Heat 1 tbsp. olive oil in a small pan and fry the minced beef and onion for 5 minutes or until the meat is browned, the onions softened. Add the oregano, cinnamon and garlic and cook for a further minute.

- Stir in the red wine and the tomatoes. Simmer gently until all the liquid has been absorbed. Season, to taste with a little sugar, salt and pepper. Stir in the cheese (optional). Set aside.

- Now make the sauce: melt the butter in a small pan over a medium heat. Blend in the flour, cooking and stirring for 30 seconds or so to lightly brown the floury paste. Gradually blend in the milk to form a smooth, creamy sauce.

- Remove from the heat and whisk in the egg yolks, a good pinch of nutmeg and salt and pepper, to taste.

- To assemble the dish, spread the meat mixture over each half aubergine to within 1 cm of the edge. Spoon on the Béchamel sauce and sprinkle each with cheese. Bake for 15-20 minutes or until piping hot and golden.

Kasia Moutuszewske

Serves 4

1 large head of green cabbage

FOR THE FILLING:
1 tbsp. olive oil
300g lean minced lamb
2 tsp. dried oregano
½ tsp. paprika
100g feta cheese, crumbled, plus
    extra to garnish
125g dried couscous
4 spring onions, finely chopped

FOR THE TOMATO SAUCE:
1 tbsp. olive oil
400g can chopped tomatoes
1 clove of garlic, finely sliced
1 red onion, finely chopped
Sea salt and freshly ground
    black pepper

Stuffed Cabbage Leaves

As a child, Kasia remembers her grandmother making this dish to serve the family for lunch every Sunday. Since then, the recipe has been passed on to Kasia by her own mother.

- Blanch the cabbage, stalk end up in a large pan of boiling water for 5-8 minutes. Drain and leave it to cool.

- Working with the cabbage stalk end up, use a sharp knife to remove the outer leaves from the main stalk, peeling them off one by one until you have 8 nice- sized leaves. (Chill the blanched centre to use another time)

- Heat the olive oil in a small pan and cook the minced lamb until browned and crumbly. Add 1 tsp. oregano and half the paprika and stir-fry for a minute or two. Remove from the heat, cool a little then stir in the feta.

- Make up the couscous according to the pack instructions. Whilst warm, stir in the remaining oregano and chopped spring onion.

- Mix the couscous with the minced lamb. Season to taste with plenty of black pepper and a little salt.

- Make a V-shaped cut to remove the thickest part of the stalk from base of each cabbage leaf.

- Place 2 heaped tbsps. of the meat mixture in the centre of each leaf, fold in the sides and roll the leaf up tightly.

- Pack the rolled leaves close together in a shallow wide saucepan. Pour boiling water around the side of the pan to come halfway up the cabbage rolls. Cover and simmer for 20 minutes.

- Make the tomato sauce; simply simmer all the ingredients in a small lidded pan for 15 minutes, adding a drop of water if required.

- Drain and serve the cabbage rolls with a little tomato sauce and extra crumbled feta.

Georgios Michailidis

Chickpea Kefte with Potato and Basil

This is Head Chef George's grandmother's recipe. It is one to pass down the line as a firm favourite and for good reason, because it's incredibly moreish and a great non-meat kefte. Shape into small round kefte or larger patties and pile into split soft burger buns topped with tomato and onion slices. Or enjoy meze style with tomato and tzatziki (see page 37) rolled up in salad leaves or flat-bread.

Serves 4 (makes 20 kefte)

400g cooked chickpeas and
   400g lentils
50g fresh white breadcrumbs
350g boiled potatoes
1 clove of garlic, finely chopped
1 tsp. dry basil leaves
1 tbsp. small capers
6 tbsp. freshly chopped flat-leaf
   parsley
6 spring onions, finely chopped
Olive oil, for greasing
Sea salt and freshly ground
   black pepper

- In a large bowl, crush the potatoes with a fork to roughly mash. Mix in the chickpeas and lentils. Season to taste with salt and pepper.

- Now mix in the remaining ingredients, season again then cover and refrigerate to let the flavours develop.

- Lightly oil your hands and form the mixture to make approximately 20 round keftes. Arrange on a lightly oiled baking tray.

- Bake in a preheated oven at 200°C (fan 180°C) / Gas 6 for 15–20 minutes or until golden brown and firm. Leave to cool slightly before using a spatula to transfer to a plate for serving.

Alexandris Bezanis

Courgette & Feta Patties

Tasty, minty and with the sweet-saltiness of feta, these patties are so good. Enjoy with a tomato and onion salad or stacked onto a nest of refreshing crunchy carrot ribbons (see page 97). Perfect too formed into small patties for a meze with tzatziki.

Makes 8

500g courgettes, grated
1 red onion, finely chopped
2 spring onions, finely chopped
2 tbsp. freshly chopped mint
150g feta cheese crumbled
100g fresh white breadcrumbs
    or rusk crumbs
2 tbsp. plain flour, to dust
3 tbsp. Greek olive oil
1 tbsp. fresh, torn flat-leaf parsley,
    to garnish
Freshly ground black pepper,
    to taste
Carrot ribbons, to serve (see
    page 97)

- Let the grated courgette sit in a colander over a large bowl to drain away the excess moisture. Then pat dry with absorbent kitchen towel. Tip into a large bowl.

- Evenly mix in the onion, spring onions, mint, crumbled feta and breadcrumbs. Season with a little black pepper.

- Form into 8 patties then gently dust with the plain flour. Set aside until ready to cook.

- Heat the oil in a large frying pan over a medium heat. Cook 3–4 patties at a time, frying for 4–5 minutes on each side, carefully turning when crisp and well coloured. Transfer to a warm plate or oven whilst you cook the remaining patties.. Serve warm topped with a scattering of fresh parsley.

Timoteo Silva

Serves 4

400g salt cod, soaked overnight
    in water
400ml full-fat milk
4 tbsp. olive oil
1 large onion, chopped
2 tbsp. plain flour
1kg large waxy potatoes
Freshly grated nutmeg
150ml double cream, lightly
    whipped
75g kefalotyri cheese, grated
    (or Cheddar-style cheese)
Sea salt and freshly ground
    black pepper

Bacalhau a Timoteo

Salt cod is dried, salted cod that needs to be rehydrated and de-salted before use. Looking like a dried-up leather shoe, it soon softens once rehydrated and is really tasty when cooked. It is extremely popular in Mediterranean countries and particularly Portugal, where it's known as bacalhau. Often eaten Tapas style, this recipe has an affinity with Greek Meze and is delicious with salad or grilled vegetables.

- Rinse the fish in several changes of fresh water after soaking overnight. Place the fish in a saucepan and pour over the milk. Bring the milk just to the boil then reduce the heat and simmer for 8 minutes. Lift the fish onto a plate and strain the milk into a jug.

- Heat 2 tbsp. oil in the pan, then add the onion and cook for 5 minutes or until softened but not coloured. Flake in the fish and cook gently for a minute or two, then sprinkle on the flour, stir with the fish and gradually blend in the reserved milk, stirring occasionally, until the sauce has thickened. Do not worry if the fish breaks up.

- Meanwhile cut the potato into 2cm cubes. Heat the remaining oil in a large sauté pan and fry the potatoes in the oil, tossing frequently, until golden and cooked through. Drain the potatoes and fold into the fish mixture. Season to taste, with salt and pepper and a little grated nutmeg.

- Spread the mixture into a shallow oblong gratin dish, top with a layer of the whipped cream and sprinkle on the cheese. Bake in a preheated oven at 200°C (fan 180°C) / Gas 6 for 20 minutes or until the surface is golden brown.

Vicky Koukia

Serves 6

6 boneless salmon fillets (each
    approx. 130g)
Zest and juice of 1 lemon
1 tsp. dried oregano
1 head of lettuce i.e. cos,
    romaine or other soft, flat
    variety
4 spring onions
1 generous bunch of flat-leaf
    parsley, chopped
1 small bunch of fresh dill,
    chopped
6 tbsp. Greek olive oil
Sea salt and freshly ground
    black pepper, to taste
Lemon wedges, to serve

Oven-Baked Salmon with Herbs

Vicky says: 'This recipe comes from my lovely mpampa (dad) and so every time I go back to my family, he has this waiting on the table for me. It's a really tasty fish dish with Omega 3, the best kind of fat you can find in food...'

- Lay the salmon in a large shallow dish. Drizzle on half of the lemon zest and juice, the oregano and salt and pepper to taste. Cover and leave to marinade in a cool place.

- Meanwhile shred the lettuce and spring onions into a large bowl, mix together with the parsley, dill, remaining lemon zest and juice and enough olive oil to make a rough paste.

- Cut six pieces of greaseproof paper or baking foil into sheets approx. 36 x 36cm or large enough to fold into a parcel around each fillet.

- Place a salmon fillet in the centre of the foil square. Evenly spread with some herby paste, drizzle on a little more olive oil and season to taste. Repeat with the remaining salmon.

- Carefully bring two sides of the parcel together, folding them over to seal the edges to make a kind of tent. Now twist the ends to seal the parcel.

- Place on a baking sheet and cook in a preheated oven 210°C (fan 200°C) / Gas 7 for 25 minutes or until the fish is tender.

- Transfer to individual plates for your guests to unwrap with care as the wafting aromatic steam will be hot. Perfect accompanied with new potatoes and a tomato salad.

Subas Pant

Serves 2

2 skinless, boneless chicken thighs
   (approx. 250g total weight)
4 tbsp. Greek olive oil
Juice of 1 lemon
A large pinch of dried chilli
   flakes
300g salad potatoes e.g..
   Charlotte, halved
1 head of broccoli, cut into
   florets
1 medium onion, cut into chunks
1 red pepper, deseeded and
   chopped
1 tbsp. freshly torn basil
50g walnuts, coarsely chopped
50g feta cheese
A large pinch of ground fennel
Sea salt and freshly ground
   black pepper, to taste

Chicken & Broccoli Salad

Every day, we quickly toss together fresh ingredients to make this deliciously wholesome salad.

- In a small dish, toss together the chicken thighs with 2 tbsp. olive oil, half the lemon juice, the chilli flakes with a little salt and pepper, to taste. Cover and marinate in a cool place for 30 minutes or so.

- Meanwhile, boil the potatoes until just tender, adding the broccoli 5 minutes before the potatoes are done. Tip the vegetables into a colander and refresh under cold running water. Drain thoroughly and tip into a large bowl. Set aside.

- Heat 1 tbsp. oil in a frying pan and cook the onions until just softened. Add to the vegetables together with the red pepper, basil and walnuts.

- Drain the chicken from its marinade and fry (or griddle), turning halfway through cooking, for 10–12 minutes, or until golden and cooked through, with all juices running clear. Cut into thick slices.

- Now toss the warm chicken in with the vegetables. Add any remaining lemon juice and olive oil (including juices from the hot pan), walnuts and seasoning to taste.

- Divide between 2 plates, crumble on the feta and finish with a sprinkling of ground fennel. Enjoy!

Ferit Akkus

Ali Nazik Kebab

'This southern Turkish speciality is a feast for all the senses. Smoky aubergine and garlicky yoghurt purée are topped with tender lamb. Enjoy this delicious kebab served with roasted or chargrilled vegetables and plain rice.'

Serves 2

FOR THE EGGPLANT AND YOGHURT PURÉE:

4 medium aubergines
250g thick whole-milk yoghurt
   (i.e. Fage brand)
2 cloves of garlic, crushed and
   finely diced

FOR THE LAMB STEW

200g lean diced lamb or minced
   meat of your choice
1 onion, chopped
2 tsp. red pepper paste or 1 tsp.
   dried chilli flakes (optional)
1 tbsp. tomato purée

FOR THE ROASTED VEGETABLES:

3 tomatoes, quartered
1 each of green, yellow and
   red pepper, deseeded and
   quartered
1 onion, quartered, root intact

Olive oil, for cooking
Freshly chopped flat-leaf
   parsley or oregano to garnish
Sea salt and freshly ground
   black pepper

- Prepare the eggplants: place directly over an open flame on the burner or in a hot griddle pan set over a medium heat and dry roast or chargrill for 15-20 minutes, turning occasionally, until all sides are cooked evenly and the skin is nicely charred, the flesh soft.

- Transfer to a colander to cool then peel and discard the skins, leaving the flesh in the colander to drain its bitter juices. Squeeze the flesh gently to help drain as much water as possible.

- Chop the eggplant, mix in the garlic, season with salt and pepper, cover and set aside until required.

- Meanwhile prepare the vegetables: spread the onions, tomato and peppers in a large tray, drizzle with olive oil, season well with salt and pepper and roast in a preheated oven 200°C (180°C fan) / Gas 6 for 25-30 minutes. For the lamb stew, heat 1 tbsp. olive oil in a wide heavy pan, add the onion and lamb and stir – fry for 5 minutes or until the lamb has browned and the onions softened.

- Add the red pepper paste or chilli (optional) and tomato purée with 2 tbsp water. Mix well, reduce the heat, cover and simmer for 20 minutes or until the lamb is tender.

- Just before serving, heat 1 tbsp. olive oil in a pan and gently reheat the eggplant purée. Remove from the heat and stir in the yogurt. Season to taste.

- Spread the eggplant and garlic purée onto two shallow plates, top with the tender meat and sauce, scatter with fresh chopped herbs.

Glauce Pela Sparsis

Loukaniko and Orzo

Serves 4

500g orzo pasta

4 tbsp. extra virgin Greek olive
  oil, plus extra, for serving

1 small onion, finely chopped

2 loukaniko sausages, sliced or
  cubed

2 cloves of garlic, finely chopped

300ml double cream

A fistful of finely chopped flat-
  leaf parsley

A fistful of finely chopped dill

A fistful of finely chopped spring
  onions

Sea salt and freshly ground
  black pepper, to taste

Glauce says: 'When I was a kid I was always watching cooking programmes and later I would try to cook. I believe this recipe comes from my Nona and Nono. I have Italian heritage and I'm inspired by Italian food. One day, I asked my staff if they wanted to try something different and they said yes, so I put on the chef's jacket and started to cook for them. Everyone really enjoyed it so once a week I am asked by the staff to make a special recipe. This was one of my creations. I hope you enjoy it!'

- Bring 4 litres of water to the boil in a large pan. Add a good pinch of salt, stir in the orzo pasta and cook for 12-14 minutes, or according to the packet instructions. Drain thoroughly and set aside.

- Heat 3 tbsp. extra virgin olive oil in a large pan, add the onion and fry until softened and golden. Then add the loukaniko sausage and cook for 3-4 minutes or until the sausage is well coloured and crisp. Add the garlic and cook for a further minute.

- Pour in the cream, reduce the heat and simmer for 2 minutes, then stir in the orzo and reheat the pasta, stirring for 2–3 minutes.

- Transfer the creamy pasta mixture into a warmed serving dish. Sprinkle with the chopped herbs and spring onions. Drizzle on a little more olive oil and some ground black pepper to taste, then serve pronto!

Kitchen note: if you cannot buy loukaniko, substitute with chorizo or a lightly spiced, cured sausage of your choice.

Dimitrios Kammos

Makes 8

1 kg lean minced beef
1 large red onion, finely chopped
1 tbsp. freshly chopped coriander
1 tsp. dried oregano
¼ tsp. ground allspice
½ tsp. ground cumin
50g feta cheese, crumbled
75g cracker crumbs or stale
   breadcrumbs
2 eggs, beaten
1 tbsp. Greek olive oil
2 sundried tomatoes, cut into
   strips
Sea salt and freshly ground
   black pepper, to taste
Soft, flat lettuce, to serve
Tzatziki (see page 37), to serve

Stuffed Burgers

Dimitrios says: 'When I first made 'stuffed burgers' I was 13 years old. I worked in a restaurant in Thessaloniki and the head chef wanted a new dish that would be different to other restaurants. I had an idea to make the 'stuffed burger'. Customers loved this delicious and tasty Greek *bifteki*. I've now decided to give it a new name...The Real Greek Burger!'

- In a large bowl, work together the beef, onion, coriander, oregano, allspice and cumin. Season with salt and pepper.

- Now evenly mix in the feta and crumbs. Add enough beaten egg to bind the ingredients together.

- Divide into 8 equal pieces and form into round patties. Cover and chill until required.

- Either pan-fry or grill the burgers, basting with a little oil if required, for 7–8 minutes on each side or until the meat juices run clear and the burger is firm when lightly pressed with fingertips. If preferred, cook in a hot oven 200°C (fan 180°C) / Gas 6 for 15 minutes or until cooked through.

- Serve either on a bed of vegetables or in a soft bun, with lettuce, sundried tomatoes and a dollop of tzatziki. It's delicious eaten hot or cold.

Kostas Kyriakou

Yiayia's Beef with Aubergine and Potatoes

Serves 4–6

6 tbsp. Greek extra virgin olive
    oil
1 tbsp. red wine
1.5kg casserole beef i.e. chuck,
    cut into chunks
1 red onion
2 cloves of garlic
1 generous pinch of ground
    nutmeg
2 tsp. dried oregano
400g can chopped tomatoes
200g tomato purée
1.5kg aubergines
1.5kg waxy potatoes
Sea salt and freshly ground
    black pepper

Our Soho manager Kostas loves this recipe, which comes from his grandmother.

- Heat 2 tbsp. olive oil in a heavy-based lidded saucepan and add the beef, in batches to brown. Pour in the red wine and cook for approximately 10 minutes until the meat has turned a reddish colour.

- Using a blender, purée the onions and garlic. Add to the meat with the nutmeg and oregano. Season well with salt and pepper.

- Now stir in the chopped tomatoes and tomato purée. Pour on enough water to cover the meat. Bring to a boil, then reduce the heat to a low simmer, cover and cook for 90 minutes or until the meat is just tender. Stir occasionally.

- Meanwhile, cut the aubergines and potatoes into thick slices and fry them in the remaining oil until half-cooked.

- Preheat the oven to 220°F (fan 200°C) / Gas 7. Carefully pour the meat and juices into a large baking tray. Cover with the potato and aubergine slices. Bake for 15–20 minutes until golden brown.

Tonia's Seasonal Plates

Tahini Dip

Serves 4 as meze

3 tbsp. tahini paste
2–4 cloves of garlic, crushed
Juice of 2–3 lemons
2 tbsp. olive oil
Sea salt
Freshly chopped flat-leaf
   parsley, paprika or chilli
   powder, to garnish

This has to be my favourite dip.

Rich-in-calcium sesame seeds are ground into a purée or paste we call tahini. Its flavour and adaptability make it an ideal ingredient in sauces, or for dipping or drizzling over our many vegetable or pulse-based dishes.

- Using an electric blender, whizz all the ingredients together until smooth. Blend in just enough cold water to form a consistency similar to thick pouring cream.

- Cover and chill, then serve into a small dipping bowl, drizzle on a little extra virgin olive oil and garnish with parsley and a pinch of paprika or chilli powder.

Kitchen note: Stir tahini thoroughly in the jar before using as, over time, the sesame oil will settle on the top.

Greek Minestrone Soup

Serves 4–6

1 tbsp. olive oil

2 rashers of streaky bacon, chopped

1 clove of garlic, chopped

1 red onion, finely chopped

1 large waxy potato, diced

2 carrots, chopped

2 sticks of celery, sliced

1 small leek, finely sliced

¼ tsp. coriander seeds

1 bay leaf

400g can chopped tomatoes

1 medium courgette, chopped

400g can cannellini beans, rinsed and drained

900ml hot vegetable stock

50g orzo pasta (or small macaroni)

50g curly kale, stalks removed and chopped

2 tbsp. freshly chopped coriander

5 tbsp. grated kefalotyri cheese (or a hard cheddar-style cheese)

Sea salt and freshly ground black pepper

This is another of the soups we put up on The Real Greek winter specials' board.

Minestrone soup is the basis for a great Saturday lunch in our busy household, and I can slip in whatever vegetables I need to use up without the younger boys noticing!

- Heat the oil in a large saucepan, add the bacon, fry until it starts to brown, then add the garlic, onion, potato, carrots, celery, leek, coriander seeds and bay leaf. Cover and cook over a low heat for 10 minutes to 'sweat' the vegetables, stirring occasionally.

- Add the tomatoes, courgette, cannellini beans and hot stock. Cover and simmer for 15–20 minutes, then add the pasta and kale. Simmer for a further 10 minutes or until the pasta is just cooked.

- Stir in the coriander, adjust the seasoning to taste, then ladle into warmed bowls. Hand around some grated cheese to melt into the soup.

Chickpea and Cumin Soup

Serves 4

3 tsp. cumin seeds
A pinch of dried chilli flakes
3 tbsp. olive oil
1 red onion, chopped
900ml hot vegetable stock
2 x 400g cans chopped
   tomatoes
400g can chickpeas, rinsed
   and drained
2 tbsp. natural Greek yoghurt
Freshly chopped coriander,
   to garnish
Sea salt and freshly ground
   black pepper

This is a stand-by store-cupboard soup, so there's no excuse for not having something hot and nutritious to eat. It takes me back to my college days' repertoire and it's definitely one recipe I will be packing off with my daughter when she starts university. It is one that we had on The Real Greek seasonal winter specials' board. I like it smooth but if you prefer a more textured soup, just don't blitz it.

- In a large saucepan, dry-fry the cumin seeds and chilli flakes until the seeds start to jump around.

- Add the oil and onion, gently cook until the onions become transparent but not browned.

- Stir in the stock and tomatoes together with half the chickpeas. Cover, bring to the boil then simmer for 20 minutes.

- Blitz the soup to a smooth texture, adjust the seasoning and add the reserved chickpeas.

- Ladle into bowls, garnish with a swirl of yoghurt and top with fresh coriander.

Artichokes City-Style

Serves 4

100ml olive oil

10 small shallots, peeled

450g new potatoes
   (e.g. Charlotte), halved

4 carrots, sliced

2 tbsp. plain flour

Juice of 1 lemon

200ml vegetable stock

10 artichoke hearts, cut in half
   (or 400g can drained)

6 spring onions, trimmed and
   chopped

50g freshly chopped dill

Sea salt and freshly ground
   black pepper

We Greeks refer to the former Constantinople as The City, and the style of cooking that emerged from it, 'City-Style'. Artichokes City-Style is a delicious vegetarian stew with artichokes, carrots and potatoes, flavoured with lemon and dill.

Serve as a main course or a delicious side dish. This also makes a great Lenten entrée. Good with extra snipped dill to garnish and crusty bread.

- Heat half the olive oil in a large flameproof casserole dish. Add the shallots, potatoes and carrots and cook for 5 minutes.

- Sprinkle in the flour, cook for 1 minute then blend in the lemon juice, stock and remaining oil. Cover and bring to the boil, then reduce the heat to simmer for 15–20 minutes or until the potatoes are just tender. Add a drop more water if required.

- Add the artichokes, spring onions and fresh dill, and season with salt and pepper. Cover and simmer for a further 15 minutes or until the artichokes are tender.

- Serve with village bread.

Aubergine Wedges with Garlic Yoghurt

Serves 2–4

1 large aubergine, cut
    lengthways into 2cm slices

FOR THE OREGANO BATTER:
75g plain flour
150ml beer or lager
2 tsp. dried oregano
Zest of ½ lemon

FOR THE GARLIC YOGHURT:
300g Greek yoghurt
1 plump clove of garlic, crushed
1 tbsp. finely chopped dill or mint

Sea salt and freshly ground
    black pepper
Vegetable oil, for frying

These are totally irresistible, so always make more than you think you will need!

- Lay the aubergine slices in a colander and sprinkle liberally with salt. Leave for 1 hour to extract the bitter juices. Rinse and pat dry with absorbent kitchen towel.

- Whisk the batter ingredients together to make a smooth batter. Season with a little salt and pepper.

- Pour enough oil into a heavy-based deep-lidded pan to fill one-third. Slowly heat the oil to 180°C. If you drop a teaspoonful of batter into the hot oil it will bubble and rise to the surface when the oil is hot enough.

- Dip the aubergine, a slice at a time, into the batter, shake off any excess, then deep-fry in batches for 5 minutes, turning occasionally until nicely golden brown. Drain on kitchen towel.

- Make the garlic yoghurt by combining the ingredients together. Sprinkle the aubergine slices with a little more oregano and sea salt. Serve with the garlic yoghurt.

Courgette Fritters

Serves 4–6 as a starter
or meze

4 medium courgettes

FOR THE BATTER:
150g self-raising flour
175ml tepid water
1 tbsp. olive oil
1 egg yolk
Sea salt and freshly ground
    black pepper
Paprika
Lemon wedges, to serve
Vegetable oil, for frying

There is something about these delicious fritters – it is
totally impossible to stop eating them until they are all
gone! I love to serve them with tzatziki (see page 37) or
tahini (see page 127).

- Slice the courgettes into long strips, batons or diagonal
  slices.

- In a large bowl, whisk the batter ingredients together to
  make a smooth batter. Add a drop more water if it looks
  too thick. Season with a little salt and pepper.

- Pour enough oil into a heavy-based, deep-lidded pan to
  fill to one-third. Slowly heat the oil to 180°C. If you drop a
  teaspoonful of batter into the hot oil it will bubble and rise
  to the surface when the oil is hot enough.

- Fold the courgettes into the batter mix, coating them evenly.
  Then fry a few pieces at a time, first shaking off any excess
  batter before you carefully lower them into the hot oil. Fry
  for around 5 minutes, turning occasionally until crisp and
  golden. Drain on kitchen towel.

- Sprinkle the courgettes with some sea salt and a dusting of
  paprika. Serve with lemon wedges.

New Potatoes with Tangy Yoghurt and Mint Dressing

Serves 4

100ml Greek yoghurt
Juice of ½ a lemon
1 clove of garlic, crushed
    (optional)
3 tbsp. finely chopped mint
500g new potatoes or salad
    potatoes (e.g. Charlotte), skin
    on
Sea salt and freshly ground
    black pepper

This side is good to eat warm with simply cooked fish or grilled meats. It's delicious cold too as a potato salad.

- Mix the yoghurt, lemon juice, garlic and mint together preferably 6 hours or so before using to let the flavours combine together for a delicious dressing. Let it come up to room temperature again before using.

- Boil the potatoes until just tender, drain thoroughly and season with a little salt and pepper. Tip into a shallow bowl and pour on the yoghurt dressing.

Feta Saganaki

Serves 2–4 as meze

200g feta cheese
1 egg
1 heaped tsp. finely chopped
  oregano
8 tbsp. plain flour
2–3 tbsp. olive oil
2 tomatoes, sliced
1 lemon, cut into wedges
Freshly ground black pepper

In Greek cuisine, saganaki is any one of a variety of dishes prepared in a small two-handled pan, the best-known being a meltingly delicious appetizer of fried cheese. Halloumi and kasseri work well, but I like to use feta and serve it with lots of lemon, fresh tomatoes on the side and crispy pitta bread.

- Slice the feta in half. Beat the egg in a shallow dish with the oregano and a little ground black pepper. Measure out the flour onto a plate.

- Dip the feta slice in the egg, shake off the excess and then dip into the flour, dusting both sides with a light coating. Repeat with the remaining slice.

- Heat some olive oil in a small frying pan or a saganaki. Fry the cheese until golden brown on both sides, with a nice crust forming. Drain on absorbent kitchen paper.

- Plate up with slices of tomato, plenty of freshly ground black pepper and wedges of lemon.

Feta Cheese Parcels with Honey and Sesame

Serves 4–6 as a starter or meze

8 leaves filo pastry
5 tbsp. olive oil
8 tbsp. Greek thyme honey
2 tbsp. sesame seeds, plus extra, to serve
4 x 100g pieces feta cheese
3 tbsp. ouzo

We put this recipe on the menu as it is a favourite of Nabil's. When I recently made it for a pop-up event at The Real Greek Marylebone, I noticed there were a few extra servings making their way to his table...

I serve these flaky cheese pies as part of a meze. They can also be made with unsalted anari cheese which is similar to ricotta cheese and so perfect for a dessert.

- Preheat the oven to 180°C (fan 160°C) / Gas 4.

- Place one sheet of filo pastry on a large baking sheet, brush with olive oil then lie another sheet directly on top. Lay a piece of feta in the centre, drizzle on 1 tbsp. honey and sprinkle with some sesame seeds.

- Fold the filo pastry around the cheese, making a secure parcel. Brush with some more oil. Repeat to make four parcels and evenly space them out on the tray. Bake in the oven for around 20–30 minutes or until golden.

- In a small pan, heat together the remaining honey and ouzo with 3 tbsp. water until just hot.

- Transfer each cooked parcel onto individual plates, cut in half and drizzle with the warm honey sauce and a final scattering of sesame seeds. Serve immediately.

Baked Pitakia with Feta, Fig and Rocket

Makes 4

6 tbsp. olive oil
3 red onions, sliced
2 tbsp. demerara sugar
6 pitakia (round pitta breads)
6 fresh figs, sliced or quartered
200g feta cheese
Fresh sprigs of thyme
Rocket salad, to serve

These chewy, soft flatbreads are topped with sweet onion, salty cheese and figs. It's lovely with a peppery rocket salad.

- Preheat the oven to 200°C (fan 180°C) / Gas 6. Lightly oil a large baking sheet.

- Heat the oil in a heavy-based saucepan, add the onions and sugar, and cook over a low heat until the onions are very soft and caramelised. Do not allow the onions to burn. This can be done up to 2 days ahead and kept chilled.

- Spread a heaped tablespoon of the onions onto each flatbread. Arrange the figs on top. Crumble the feta over and scatter with the thyme.

- Transfer to the baking tray and cook for 12–15 minutes or until the cheese is tinged golden. Serve straight away with a rocket salad on the side.

Chickpea Feta Salad

Serves 4

1 small red onion, finely sliced
1 red chilli, deseeded and finely
    chopped
4 ripe tomatoes, cut into bite
    sized chunks
Juice of 1 lime
3 tbsp. extra virgin olive oil
410g canned chickpeas, drained
1 tbsp. freshly chopped mint
1 tbsp. freshly chopped flat-leaf
    parsley or coriander
100g feta cheese
Sea salt and freshly ground
    black pepper

Whilst I love the convenience of canned chickpeas, the nutty bite of home-soaked and cooked chickpeas are worth the effort. This is also good made with white cannellini or flageolet beans...

- Place the onion, chilli and tomatoes in a large bowl with half the lime juice, the olive oil and some salt and plenty of freshly ground black pepper, to taste.

- Heat the chickpeas with a drop of oil in a small pan to just warm through, then add all but a couple of tablespoons to the bowl. Mash the remaining chickpeas and add these too...this will add a creamy consistency.

- Stir in the mint and parsley together with the remaining lime juice, if needed.

- Crumble on the feta and the salad is ready, best served at room temperature.

Cretan-style Orange Salad

Serves 4

4 small cooked beetroot, cubed

Juice of 1 small lemon

6 tbsp. extra virgin olive oil,
  or to taste

3 large navel oranges

1 large bunch watercress,
  sprigs only

200g feta cheese

2 tsp. dried oregano, or 2 tbsp.
  freshly chopped

12 green and black Greek olives
  drained

Sea salt and freshly ground
  black pepper, to taste

The island of Crete is, according to folklore, the birthplace of watercress. We Greeks use this peppery plant in a variety of classic dishes including this traditional colourful salad. I like to add rocket and spinach too when in season.

- Combine the beetroot, most of the lemon juice, 2 tbsp. olive oil and salt and pepper in a glass bowl. Cover and set aside.

- Peel the oranges, cutting away any white pith with a small, sharp knife. Slice each orange segment out onto a plate, leaving behind the pithy membrane.

- Place the watercress in a shallow serving bowl, then add the beetroot and orange. Combine together before crumbling on the feta.

- Now scatter on the oregano and olives, drizzle on the remaining lemon juice and olive oil, and season to taste with some more freshly ground black pepper.

Cretan Dakos Salad

Serves 4

4 small barley rusks
1 small red onion, finely chopped
1 red chilli, deseeded and finely sliced
200g ripe tomatoes, roughly chopped (or use cherry tomatoes, halved)
Juice of 1 lemon
4 tbsp. extra virgin olive oil
100g feta cheese
1 tsp. dried oregano
12–16 kalamata olives, chopped
Sea salt and freshly ground black pepper

Dakos, also known as twice-baked bread, is a Cretan speciality, a hard rusk used like a big crouton or bruschetta topped with a tomato, cheese and a lemony olive oil 'ladolemono'. My dako often collapses under the weight of eating it with my eyes as I pile the rusk high, while the dressing soaks down and causes an avalanche. It's messy to eat but delicious!

- Mix together the onion, chilli, tomato, lemon juice, olive oil, a pinch of salt and some freshly ground black pepper. Leave this 'salsa' to stand for 15 minutes or so for the flavours to develop.

- When ready to serve, quickly dip each dako into water to just moisten. Place in the centre of a plate, splash on a drop of ladolemono (see page 87), then pile the tomato mixture on top.

- Crumble a healthy layer of feta over the tomato top, sprinkle with oregano and olives. Enjoy.

Warm Halloumi and Peach Salad

Serves 2 as a main
or 6 as a meze

3 ripe, firm peaches, halved
   and stoned
2 tbsp. olive oil
250g halloumi cheese
3 red chicory, root intact,
   quartered
1 bunch of spring onions,
   trimmed and chopped
   diagonally into 5cm slices.

FOR THE DRESSING:
1 red chilli, deseeded and finely
   chopped
½ large bunch fresh coriander,
   roughly chopped
5 tbsp. white wine vinegar
3 tbsp. clear Greek honey

This is one of my favourite salads, especially when I can pick home-grown peaches ripened to perfection under the Mediterranean sun. The saltiness of halloumi goes so well with the sweetness of the fruit. Sometimes I use fennel instead of chicory.

- First make the dressing: Place all the ingredients in a large, lidded jam jar and shake to mix well.

- Cut the peach halves into 5 wedges. Cut the cheese into 1cm slices. Heat half the oil in a large frying pan and fry the halloumi for 3-4 minutes on each side or until a golden crust forms. Remove from the pan and keep warm.

- Add the chicory and spring onions to the hot oil, fry for a minute or two to lightly colour and wilt the leaves. Transfer to a plate lined with absorbent kitchen towel.

- Add the remaining oil to the pan and fry the peaches over a high heat for 1 minute just to soften and colour slightly.

- Now gently combine all the prepared ingredients onto a big plate and fold in the dressing.

Warm Pomegranate and Bulgur Wheat Salad

Serves 4

1 tbsp. olive oil

½ medium butternut squash, cut into rough 2cm cubes

2 courgette, halved lengthways and sliced thickly

2 cloves of garlic, crushed

1 tbsp. harissa paste

1 tsp. ground cumin

1 tsp. ground turmeric

1 red pepper, deseeded and sliced

3 tbsp. clear Greek honey

600ml hot vegetable stock

225g bulgur wheat

150g baby spinach leaves

Finely grated rind and juice 1 lemon

2 tbsp. freshly chopped mint

2 tbsp. freshly chopped coriander

4 tbsp. pomegranate seeds

Sea salt, to taste

Little pomegranate seeds shine out like hidden jewels in this big salad. Served warm, the flavours are much more intense, but it is just as good a day later! I like to use bulgur wheat, which is a whole-wheat grain that has been cracked and partially pre-cooked – it is naturally high in fibre and a great carrier of flavours too. Couscous works just as well, too.

- Heat the oil in a large wok or frying pan. Stir-fry the butternut squash for 5 minutes until nicely coloured. Add the courgette and fry for a further 2–3 minutes or until the vegetables are just tender but still with some bite.

- Meanwhile, mix together the garlic, harissa paste, cumin, turmeric and red pepper. Stir into the vegetables and cook for a further minute. Season with salt and drizzle on the honey, then set aside.

- Pour the hot stock into a pan, stir in the bulgur wheat and simmer for 15 minutes or until the grains have absorbed a lot of the liquid and are tender. Drain thoroughly and tip into a large serving bowl.

- Toss the spinach through the hot grains to wilt the leaves then fold in the vegetables and spice mix, lemon rind and juice, mint, coriander and finally the pomegranate seeds.

- Serve warm or at room temperature.

Squid and Pastoulma Salad

Serves 4 - 6 as Meze

150ml extra virgin olive oil
Juice of 2 limes
3 tbsp. red wine vinegar
2 tbsp. olive oil
200g Pastoulma, diced
500g squid, cleaned and
    chopped into rings
100g fresh watercress, tough
    stalks removed
1 tbsp. capers, rinsed and
    drained
1 tbsp. freshly chopped mint
Sea salt and freshly ground
    black pepper

A Greek equivalent of 'Surf & Turf', this really is peasant food at its best. Pastoulma, our spicy Greek sausage with its rich red oiliness is a perfect match for the squid in this salad.

- Make the dressing: Mix together the olive oil, lime juice and red wine vinegar. Season well with salt and pepper, then set aside.

- Heat the olive oil in a large frying pan over a medium heat. Add the pastoulma and fry for 3–4 minutes until it becomes brown and slightly crisp. Transfer to a large serving bowl.

- Now add the squid to the hot pan and stir-fry for 1–2 minutes or until opaque. Remove from the pan with a slotted spoon and add to the pastoulma.

- Stir the dressing into the hot pan, swirling around to warm it through.

- Now make up the salad: Toss the watercress, capers and mint into the bowl with the pastoluma and squid. Drizzle over the warm dressing. Season as required. Divide between four small serving plates.

Kitchen note: if you cannot buy Pastoulma, substitute with chorizo or a lightly spiced cured sausage of your choice.

Red Mullet Parcels

Serves 2

4 very fresh red mullet, scaled
   and gutted
3 tbsp. extra virgin olive oil
2 bay leaves
½ tbsp. rosemary leaves, freshly
   stripped from a branch
2 cloves of garlic, finely sliced
1 large lemon, sliced into 8
2 large sheets of greaseproof
   paper
Sea salt and freshly ground
   black pepper

There aren't many ingredients in this recipe, but the secret is in the cooking, with the freshest of fish and fragrant ingredients sealed in unison. Pourgouri with tomatoes, tzatziki (see page 37) or tahini (see page 127) would round this dish off nicely.

- Preheat the oven to 200°C (fan 180°C fan) / Gas 6. Wash the fish well, sprinkle inside and out with salt and leave to drain. Rinse again and pat dry on absorbent kitchen towel.

- Place 1 bay leaf in the middle of a large sheet of greaseproof paper, top with 2 fish, then sprinkle each with the rosemary, garlic and the olive oil, drizzling a little in the cavity too. Scatter slices of lemon over the fish. Repeat for the second parcel.

- Bring the wide edges of the paper together and fold down, tuck or twist the ends together to make sealed parcels with room enough for the steam to waft up around the fish. Transfer to a baking sheet and cook for 20 minutes.

- Slide the parcels onto warmed plates and serve. Let your guests have the pleasure (whilst taking care) of tearing open the parcel, homing in on the wonderful aroma and treat in store.

Tuna Kebabs with Caper Sauce

Serves 4–6

4 fresh tuna steaks (approx. 175g each), cut into chunks
2 red onions, peeled and quartered
2 red or green peppers, deseeded and cut into chunks
A squeeze of lemon
Olive oil, for basting

FOR THE CAPER SAUCE:
Juice of 1 large lemon
100ml olive oil
75g capers in brine, rinsed and chopped
1 tsp. Dijon mustard
1 tbsp. freshly chopped dill or flat-leaf parsley (optional)
Sea salt and freshly ground black pepper

Pitta breads and crunchy chopped salad, to serve

Firm fish like tuna make great kebabs cooked over hot coals. And as I love capers, this salty-sour dressing tops off the tuna perfectly. Capers are the pickled flower buds of the caper bush, which grows wild all over the Mediterranean. They are still hand-picked too...

- Place the tuna in a shallow dish with enough olive oil to lightly coat. Season with a little salt and pepper.

- Separate the onion leaves. Starting with onion, make up the kebabs, alternating with the pepper and tuna onto skewers.

- To make the caper sauce, simply shake all the ingredients together in a lidded jar.

- Cook the kebabs for 7–8 minutes over hot coals or under a preheated grill, basting with any remaining oil and a squeeze of lemon, turning once halfway through cooking. Take care not to over-cook the tuna or it will turn dry.

- Drizzle the caper sauce over the tuna and serve alongside warmed split pitta bread, stuffed with chopped salad.

Warm Tzatziki Chicken Salad

Serves 2

300g Greek yoghurt
Juice of 1 small lemon
1 small clove of garlic, crushed (optional)
A handful of freshly chopped mint, plus extra for garnish
2 tbsp. olive oil
4 boneless, skinless chicken thighs
70g rocket
1 small cucumber, cut into chunks
6 spring onions, chopped
150g crumbled feta cheese or grated kefalotyri
Sea salt and freshly ground black pepper

Also known as Zeus Salad, this warm chicken salad is my interpretation and mix of these classic Greek flavours. It works well substituting the chicken and mint with salmon and dill, too.

- Make the dressing: Mix the yoghurt, lemon juice, garlic and mint together. Season with a little salt, cover and set aside.

- Open out the chicken thighs to help to cook evenly. Heat the olive oil in a non-stick frying pan and fry the chicken for 5–6 minutes on each side until cooked through and the juices run clear.

- Divide the rocket between two shallow bowls together with the cucumber and onions. Slice the chicken and add to the salad, then spoon on the dressing.

- Scatter on the cheese, and season with plenty of ground black pepper.

Chicken Stuffed with Feta and Sundried Tomatoes

Serves 4

4 boneless, skinless chicken
    breasts
2 tbsp. olive oil
1 small red pepper, deseeded
    and finely chopped
4 cloves of garlic, finely chopped
5 large sundried tomatoes,
    diced
200g feta cheese, finely
    crumbled
30g fresh breadcrumbs (approx.
    1 thick slice)
1 tbsp. fresh chopped thyme
    leaves (or 1 tsp. dried)
Sea salt and freshly ground
    black pepper

An all-rounder, perfect party food, great for family meals and tasty eaten cold in picnics. It's a recipe you can prepare well ahead too.

- Preheat the oven to 180°C (fan 160°C) / Gas 4.

- Lay the chicken breasts between two large sheets of clingfilm. Use a rolling pin to pound them out to approx. 1cm thickness.

- Heat the olive oil in a pan and cook the pepper and garlic for 2 minutes, just to soften. Set aside to cool.

- In a bowl, combine the tomatoes, feta, breadcrumbs and thyme. Add the pepper and garlic with some of the pan juices to moisten.

- Spoon a quarter of the stuffing mix onto each chicken breast, then roll up as tightly as you can, like making a burrito. Use a couple of cocktail sticks or butcher's string to secure.

- Place the chicken on a greased baking sheet, and brush with olive oil. Season with a little salt and pepper. Cook for 30–35 minutes. Leave to stand for 5 minutes before slicing through and serving.

Yiayia's Chicken Kokkinisto

Serves 4

4 tbsp. Greek olive oil

1.6kg chicken thighs, skin on, bone in

1 large onion, roughly chopped

250ml Greek red wine

4 tbsp. tomato purée diluted in 450ml hot water

1 large piece of cassia bark (or cinnamon)

4 whole allspice berries

2 bay leaves

Sea salt and freshly ground black pepper

Saffron rice to serve (see page 83)

My favourite Kokkinisto – again passed down through the generations. Using a variety of herbs and spices that work well with succulent chicken thigh, it is a light yet flavoursome stew. It's delicious accompanied with fragrant saffron rice (see page 83).

- Heat the oil over a medium heat in a large flameproof lidded casserole dish. Gently cook the chicken skin-side down for 10 minutes or until browned. Remove with a slotted spoon and set aside.

- Add the onion to the hot oil and cook for 5 minutes or until softened but not coloured.

- Return the chicken to the pan, pour over the wine and simmer for 5 minutes to reduce by half. Then add the tomato purée liquid, spices and bay leaves.

- Season well, cover and simmer for 1 hour or until the chicken is tender. Serve with saffron rice.

Chicken with Lemons

Serves 4

8 large chicken thighs, skin on,
  on the bone
6 tbsp. Greek olive oil
1 head of garlic
2 large red onions
2 lemons
250ml dry white wine
Sea salt, to taste
150g Kalamata or Greek
  green olives
Flat leaf parsley, to garnish

Succulent chicken thigh roasted with lemon and olives – quick to put together and simply cooked using the best Greek ingredients. This is such a simple dish to make, I like to serve it with a big green salad and some Greek village bread.

- Heat the oven to 180°C (fan 160°C).

- Drizzle a generous layer of olive oil onto the bottom of a roasting dish or oven tray, rub the chicken in the oil and then arrange skin side up.

- Break the garlic into cloves. Peel the onions and leaving the root intact, cut into large wedges. Cut the lemons into wedges.

- Scatter the garlic, onion and lemon wedges in around the chicken. Pour on the wine, swirling the tin to mix well. Season with sea salt.

- Cook for 45 minutes then add the olives and cook for a further 10-15 minutes or until the chicken skin is crispy and all juices run clear.

- Transfer the chicken to a warm platter, place the roasting tin over a low heat and bubble the juices for 5 minutes to reduce a little. Pour over the chicken, garnish with plenty of fresh parsley and serve.

Yoghurt-marinated Chicken Skewers

Serves 6 as meze

500g Greek yoghurt

3 cloves of garlic, finely chopped
  or grated

Juice of 1 lemon

1 tbsp. olive oil

1 tsp. sugar

1 tsp. chilli powder

2cm piece of fresh ginger,
  grated

½ tsp. ground cumin

½ tsp. ground coriander

6 boneless, skinless chicken
  thighs, cut into pieces

Sea salt, to taste

Time to marinade is all that is required for this easy recipe, and fine weather for the BBQ.

- Place all the ingredients in a large bowl and combine well using clean hands.

- Cover the bowl with clingfilm and place in the fridge overnight or for at least 6 hours to allow the flavours to develop.

- Thread the chicken onto 6–8 skewers. Discard the marinade.

- Cook the chicken skewers over medium-hot coals or under a preheated medium-heat grill for 10–12 minutes, turning once or twice and basting with oil. Or cook in a preheated oven 200°C (fan 180°C) / Gas 6 for 20–25 minutes or until cooked throughout.

- Serve with warm pitta bread, dips, olives and chopped salad.

Kitchen note: Do not thread the chicken pieces together too tightly. Leave room for the heat to penetrate and circulate around the chicken.

Beef Stifado

Serves 4–6

6 tbsp. olive oil

1.5kg lean stewing beef (e.g. chuck), cubed

1.5kg shallots, peeled

4 cloves of garlic, chopped

5 tbsp. red wine vinegar

3 cinnamon sticks or cassia bark

2 bay leaves

1 tsp. aniseed or 2 star anise or 1 tsp. fennel seeds

3 x 400g cans chopped tomatoes

Sea salt and freshly ground black pepper

This is a wonderfully aromatic dish that fills the house with warming aromas of cinnamon and aniseed. This stew is traditionally served with orzo pasta but I like to soak up the slightly sweet tomato sauce with plain rice or pourgouri.

- Heat the olive oil in a large, heavy-based lidded casserole dish. Brown the meat in batches, setting aside in a large bowl.

- Add the shallots to the hot oil and gently cook until golden and caramelised. Add the garlic and cook for a further minute before stirring in the vinegar with 300ml water, the cinnamon, bay leaves and aniseed.

- Return the meat and any juices to the pan together with the tomatoes. Stir well, bring to a steady boil, then cover, reduce the heat to low and simmer for 90 minutes or until the meat is very tender. Remove the lid for the last 20 minutes to let the sauce reduce and thicken slightly.

- Adjust the seasoning and serve. Serve with short-grain white rice.

Kleftiko

Serves 4-6

1 shoulder of lamb, cut into
  fist-sized pieces
2–3 lemons, cut into wedges
3 large bay leaves, torn
2 tsp. dried oregano or a
  handful of fresh stems
1 tsp. ground cinnamon
4 large potatoes, peeled and cut
  into quarters lengthways
3–4 cherry tomatoes (optional)
Olive oil
Sea salt and freshly ground
  black pepper, to taste

This classic dish is named after the notorious 'klephtes'
or bandits who stole mountain sheep or goats for food,
cooked in sealed pots to avoid any smoke giving them
away! A rustic dish, left to cook until the meat falls away
from the bone, I, like many Greeks, cook Kleftiko in our
clay dome oven outside, but a large roasting tin with foil to
cover works just as well in a conventional oven.

- Preheat the oven to 150°C (fan 130°C) / Gas 2.

- Rub the lamb all over with the lemon wedges and some
  oil. Place in a roasting tin with the bay leaves, oregano and
  ground cinnamon.

- Add the potatoes and tomatoes (if using). Season with
  salt and pepper. With clean hands, fold through all the
  ingredients to coat well.

- Cover with a large, double-thickness sheet of foil, sealing
  well. Roast for 2–3 hours or until the meat is falling away
  from the bone.

- Rest the Kleftiko for 10 minutes before serving with a fresh
  Greek salad and country bread.

Lamb Kofta with Spicy Tahini Dip

Serves 4–5

FOR THE KOFTA:
500g lean minced lamb
50g grated sweet potato
50g fresh breadcrumbs
   (approx. 2 slices)
50g Greek yoghurt
2 plump cloves of garlic, crushed
2 tsp. ground coriander
1 tsp. ground cumin
2 tbsp. freshly chopped mint
2 tbsp. freshly chopped
   coriander
A small bunch of flat-leaf
   parsley
Olive oil, for brushing
Sea salt and freshly ground
   black pepper

FOR THE TAHINI DIP:
200g Greek yoghurt
3 tbsp. tahini
Juice of 2 lemons
4 cloves of garlic, crushed
¼ tsp. hot chilli powder, to taste
1 tsp. salt

8 crisp lettuce leaves, to serve

Olive oil must be one of the Holy Trinity of ingredients in Greek cooking along with garlic and possibly sesame seeds. As much as I love the healthy attributes of olive oil, I like to bake kofta rather than frying it, but roasted and pressed sesame seeds make up for it, producing a robust oily paste or tahini – the basis for a wonderful dressing to dollop alongside.

- Preheat the oven to 180°C (fan 160°C) / Gas 4.

- To make the kofta, mix all the ingredients together. Season well and form into 16 balls, then cup each in your hands to shape into ovals.

- Arrange on a lightly oiled baking tray and cook for around 30 minutes, turning once after 20 minutes.

- Meanwhile make the Tahini dip. Simply beat all the ingredients together, adding 3–6 tbsp. water to slacken to a looser dip, as preferred.

- Divide the kofta between the lettuce leaves and drizzle with the dip. Roll up the leaves and enjoy.

Lamb Moussaka

Serves 4

1 tbsp. olive oil
500g lean minced lamb
2 large onions, chopped
2 cloves of garlic, chopped
2 tsp. dried oregano
4 tsp. ground cinnamon
2 tbsp. tomato purée
200g can chopped tomatoes
    or passata
200ml red wine
1 large baking potato,
    250g, finely sliced
1 large aubergine, 1cm slices
    lengthways
2 courgettes, 1 cm slices
    lengthways
For the béchamel sauce:
25g butter
25g plain flour
300ml milk
A pinch of ground nutmeg
Salt and freshly ground black
    pepper

There are so many variations of this Greek comfort dish that I get quite giddy! But this is mine and I like to include more vegetables and more cinnamon than usual; if it is not for you, then halve the quantity.

- Heat the olive oil in a pan and add the minced lamb, onions and oregano. Cook for 5 minutes until the meat is brown and crumbly, and the onions have softened. Now add the garlic and cook for a further minute, then stir in the cinnamon and season with salt and pepper.

- Stir in the chopped tomatoes or passata, the tomato purée and red wine. Cover and simmer for 20 minutes.

- Make the sauce: Melt the butter over a medium heat in a small saucepan. Blend in the flour and continue to cook, stirring for 30 seconds or so to lightly brown the flour to a paste. Gradually blend in the milk, a little at a time, whisking to form a smooth, creamy sauce. Add a little grated nutmeg and season to taste.

- Spread half the meat in the base of a shallow oblong ovenproof dish (about 28 x 20 x 6cm deep), then layer with potato, aubergine, courgette, the minced lamb, potato, courgette and finally aubergine. Do not worry if the layers are not equal.

- Pour over the béchamel sauce, then pop into a preheated oven at 180°C (fan 160°C) / Gas 4 and cook for 35–45 minutes or until the top is golden brown. Serve with salad on the side.

Lamb stuffed with Dates

Serves 8

2 tbsp. olive oil
2 onions, finely sliced
150g chopped dates
1 boned, butterflied leg of lamb
4 cloves of garlic, finely sliced
4 tbsp. chopped flat-leaf parsley
2 tsp. ground cumin
1 tsp. ground cinnamon
125g sundried tomatoes
150ml red wine
3 tbsp. tomato purée
125g whole dates
Sea salt and freshly ground
    black pepper
Thinly sliced, crisp, roasted
    potatoes, to serve

This recipe is a wonderful alternative to a plain Sunday roast; it is wonderful as a dinner party centrepiece, too.

My children love lamb and this roast is no exception. I stuff a boned leg of lamb with sweet chopped dates, earthy spices like cumin and robust sundried tomatoes. The end result is simply delicious.

- Heat the olive oil in a pan. Fry the onions and chopped dates for 5 minutes to soften. Add the garlic, parsley and spices and cook for a further minute. Stir in the parsley.

- Open the lamb out onto a board and spoon the date mixture down the centre. Top with a layer of sundried tomatoes. Season with salt and pepper.

- Wrap the lamb around the stuffing and secure firmly with string. Transfer to a roasting dish.

- Whisk together the red wine and tomato purée, pour over the lamb. Cover with foil and cook in a preheated oven at 180°C (fan 160°C) / Gas 4 for 2 hours or until very tender.

- Remove the foil, add a little extra red wine or water to the roasting dish if required, and scatter in the whole dates. Return to the oven for a further 20 minutes.

- Serve the lamb in thick slices on a bed of thinly sliced crisp roasted potatoes with the rich pan juices spooned alongside.

Desserts and Drinks

Baklava

Makes: 11–12 pieces

FOR THE SYRUP:
300g caster sugar
Juice of ½ lemon
300g clear Greek honey

FOR THE FILLING:
150g caster sugar
25g ground cinnamon
500g walnuts, finely chopped

2 pkt. filo pastry (550g total)
500g ghee, melted
100g fine semolina
1 tbsp. whole cloves

Baklava is a very rich, sweet pastry so typical of the Middle East and particularly Greece. It's made from layers of filo pastry filled with chopped nuts, and held together with syrup or honey. A tiny piece is quite enough! It's wonderful with a dark strong cup of Greek coffee.

- Make the syrup: Pour 500ml water into a saucepan with the sugar and lemon juice. Bring to a steady boil, then add the honey. Simmer for 40-50 minutes. Remove from heat. The syrup is now ready to use. It will store well in a screw-top jar in the fridge if made ahead.

- Make the filling: Blend the sugar, ground cinnamon and walnuts together in a food processor or use a hand-held blender until mixed. The nuts should be finely chopped but not sandy.

- Now make the Baklava: grease a shallow oblong baking tray the size of, or slightly smaller than, the filo sheets with some melted ghee. Layer 6–7 sheets of filo pastry into the tin, brushing each layer with the ghee and a fine dusting of semolina.

- Now spread some filling mix over the top pastry sheet to cover, then add 3 more filo sheets, buttering and dusting as before, some more filling and then repeating with 3 more sheets until all the filling mixture is used up. Top with the remaining pastry sheets. Allow the pastry to rest in a cool place for 1 hour before cutting into 24 equal diamond or triangle pieces, piercing each piece with a clove.

- Cook in a preheated oven at 180°C (fan 160°C) / Gas 4 for 45 minutes or until the filo is golden and crisp.

- Pour the cold syrup over the hot pastry letting it flow evenly between the slices. Leave to soak up for 30 minutes before serving with a drizzle of any remaining syrup.

Bougasta

Makes: 15–18 pies

75g fine semolina
100g caster sugar
2 tbsp. rosewater
¼ tsp. ground mastic
3 sheets of puff pastry
1 egg, beaten
50g icing sugar or ground
   cinnamon for dusting
Vegetable oil, for deep frying
Vanilla ice cream, to serve

A traditional dessert from Northern Greece, these crisp pastry pies are filled with a rose-scented semolina paste. They are lovely eaten warm with a generous scoop of vanilla ice cream.

- Pour 500ml water into a saucepan and bring to a steady boil. Pour in the semolina, sugar, rosewater and mastic, stirring well.

- Reduce the heat to simmer for 5 minutes or until the semolina mixture has thickened. Spoon the mixture into a bowl and leave to cool.

- Cut each pastry sheet in half and then cut each half into 3 rectangles.

- Lightly flour a clean work surface. Roll out a rectangle, place a heaped teaspoon of the semolina mixture in the middle, but slightly off centre. Brush the pastry edges with egg then fold over and seal the edges together using a fork.

- Repeat with the remaining pastry to make up all the pies. Meanwhile, pour enough oil into a heavy-based deep-lidded pan to fill to one-third. Slowly heat the oil to the correct frying temperature.

- Deep-fry the pastries in batches, until golden and crisp. Drain on absorbent kitchen towels. Serve immediately, dusted with icing sugar and ground cinnamon, and with a scoop of vanilla ice cream on top.

Semolina Cake

Makes: 10–12 pieces

FOR THE SYRUP:

400g caster sugar

3 large pieces of cussia bark or
    cinnamon quills

7 cloves

Juice of ½ lemon

Large glug of brandy

FOR THE CAKE:

5 free-range medium eggs,
    beaten

200g caster sugar

200ml light olive oil

Zest and juice of 1 large orange

500g fine semolina

2 tsp. mastic or 1 tbsp. orange
    blossom water

3 tsp. baking powder

Whole blanched almonds,
    to decorate

As with all good Greek desserts, there is a syrup to steep this semolina cake in. And for flavour I like to use mastic, which is a tree resin taken from trees grown only on the island of Hios – and is an acquired flavour used in ice cream. You can substitute it with vanilla extract, orange blossom water or rosewater.

- Make the syrup: Place the sugar, cinnamon and cloves in a pan with the lemon juice and 400ml cold water. Bring to the boil, reduce the heat to a steady simmer for 15–20 minutes. Remove from the heat and leave to cool.

- Preheat the oven to 170°C (fan 150°C) / Gas 4. Lightly grease a 23cm round or square, loose-bottomed cake tin or as Greeks would use, a shallow, square ovenproof glass dish.

- In a large bowl, whisk the eggs and sugar together until light and fluffy then blend in the olive oil and orange zest and juice before folding in the semolina. Crush the mastic with a pinch of sugar in a pestle and mortar (the sugar prevents the mastic from becoming too sticky). Stir in to the mixture with the baking powder.

- Transfer to the prepared tin and arrange the almonds on the top. Bake for 45 minutes or until golden, well-risen and springy to the touch.

- Set the hot cake tin onto a shallow plate and ladle the cold syrup over the top. Let the cake soak up the syrup for 30 minutes or so before removing from the tin. Store in an airtight container in a cool place.

Daktila

Makes: 25–30

750g plain flour
100ml sunflower oil or light
    olive oil
1 tsp. salt
For the syrup:
200g caster sugar
1 tsp. lemon juice
4 sticks of cinnamon bark
Groundnut oil, for deep frying

FOR THE FILLING:

700g whole blanched almonds,
    finely chopped in a food
    processor
200g caster sugar
4 tsp. ground cinnamon
100ml rosewater

The Greeks use a lot of home-produced nuts in their desserts, like daktila, or as I call them Almond Lady Fingers. Like many other Greek sweet pastries, daktila are deliciously fragrant with rose water and cinnamon, and of course, they are very sweet!

- Make the syrup: Place the ingredients in a small saucepan with 200ml cold water. Bring to a steady boil for 5 minutes. Take off the heat to cool.

- Meanwhile make the dough by mixing the flour, oil and salt together, crumbling with your fingers to form breadcrumbs. Gradually work in 400ml of tepid water, kneading well to make a smooth, firm dough. Wrap in clingfilm and leave to rest for 1 hour.

- For the filling, simply mix together the almonds, sugar, cinnamon and rosewater.

- To make the daktila, the pastry can be finely rolled out by hand or using a pasta machine. Divide the dough into three, covering two of the pieces with a tea towel to keep moist. Either feed the remaining dough through the machine on a thin setting (no. 1 or 2) or roll out on a lightly floured board to form a long, thin piece of dough, approximately 10cm wide.

- Take 1 tsp. of the filling, place it on the end of the dough, roll the dough over twice then cut away any overlap. Use a fork to crimp and seal both ends of the pastry, encasing the nut filling in the middle. Place each daktila onto grease-proof paper to avoid sticking. Carry on making the little parcels until you have used all the dough.

- Pour enough oil into a deep, heavy-based pan to fill one-third. Gently heat until very hot – test this by dropping a walnut-sized piece of dough in the oil; if the oil is hot enough, the dough will turn golden brown in no time.

- Use a draining spoon to slide a few daktila into the hot oil, and fry until golden brown. Drain and immediately soak in the cold syrup for one minute, then transfer to a shallow dish or plate. Repeat until all the daktila are cooked and steeped in the syrup.

Galadoboureko Milk Pudding Pie

Serves 4–6

FOR THE SYRUP:

500g caster sugar

Juice of ½ lemon

A piece of cinnamon bark

FOR THE FILLING:

3 free-range eggs

200g corn flour

1.2 litres fresh milk

200g caster sugar

6 tbsp rosewater or orange
    blossom water

175g melted unsalted butter or
    100ml groundnut oil

450g filo pastry

Known as galadoboureko, this Cypriot-style custard tart is the first proper pudding I tasted as a young child, so it's little wonder I have a sweet tooth.

- First make the syrup: Place the sugar, lemon juice and the cinnamon bark into a pan. Pour in 500ml water, stir and bring to the boil, then leave to gently bubble steadily for 10 minutes. Cool.

- For the custard filling, beat the eggs in a large bowl and blend in the corn flour with just enough milk to make a smooth paste.

- Heat the remaining milk in a saucepan until just scalding. Whisk a little of the hot milk into the paste, then pour it all back into the pan. Stir continuously over a gentle heat until the custard is smooth and coats the back of a wooden spoon.

- Stir in the sugar and rosewater. Remove from the heat.

- Preheat the oven to 150°C (130°C Fan) / Gas 2.

- Brush some melted butter or oil around the base of an oblong lasagne–style ovenproof dish. Layer half the sheets of pastry into the base of the dish, brushing each sheet with butter or oil. Pour in the custard. Cover with the remaining filo pastry, buttering in between each sheet.

- Bake for 50–60 minutes, raising the temperature a little towards the end if the pastry needs to take on more colour, but keep an eye on it.

- Remove from the oven and whilst still hot, pour the cold syrup all over the pastry. Leave for a few moments to let the syrup seep and settle. Cut into wedges and serve warm or chilled.

Kataifi

Serves 6

450g kataifi pastry strands
150g melted butter

FOR THE SYRUP:
250g caster sugar
300ml water
3 tbsp. orange blossom water

FOR THE FILLING:
225g almonds, skins on, chopped
2 tbsp. caster sugar
2 tsp. ground cinnamon
1 tbsp. orange blossom water

A glass of iced water goes well with this super-sweet pastry. I also like to eat it with a dollop of sharp Greek yoghurt. If kataifi pastry is a new ingredient to you, it is like shredded wheat! You can buy it in Middle Eastern and Greek delis. I tend to give the slab a good tap on the table to loosen and separate it well before handling.

- Make the syrup: Place the sugar and water in a saucepan. Bring to the boil then simmer steadily for 10 minutes. Stir in the orange blossom water and leave to cool.

- Mix together the ingredients for the filling, moistening with 2 tbsp. cold water.

- To make the kataifi, pull off a length of the pastry strands and spread out on the clean work surface to look like an oblong straw mat. Spoon a line of the filling along the length of the strands to just within the edge. Working away from you, roll up the kataifi, wrapping around the filling, and tucking in the ends and edges. You should end up with a long cigar shape.

- Place the kataifi into a shallow, lightly oiled baking tray. Repeat the process until the tray is filled with rolls of pastry. Sprinkle the melted butter over the top.

- Bake in a preheated oven at 180°C (fan 160°C) / Gas 4 or until crisp and golden.

- Pour the cooled syrup over the hot kataifi and leave in the baking tray to soak for half an hour before cutting and serving. It is best stored in the baking tray too.

Emma Mankarious

500g frozen kunafa (shredded filo pastry)
200g ghee
400g can of condensed milk
½ tsp. vanilla extract
50g chopped pistachio nuts

Pistachio Kunafa

These little treats are based on a Levantine cheese pastry, which is soaked in a sweet, sugar-based syrup, typical of the former Ottoman Empire. This simpler version is still 'oh so sweet' but uses condensed milk instead of syrup to bind together the shredded filo pastry. It goes really well with a glass of iced water or a strong, bitter Greek coffee.

- Shred the frozen filo pastry finely by hand into a bowl. Meanwhile, heat the ghee in a large pan.

- Carefully place handfuls of the pastry into the hot ghee to toast, moving the strands around continuously to prevent it burning.

- When the strands are golden brown, remove the pan from the heat and stir in the condensed milk and vanilla, combining well.

- Use an ice-cube tray or mini muffin tray to form each kunafa. Place a teaspoon of chopped pistachios into the base of each mould, then top with a tablespoon of kunafa mixture, pressing the mixture down with your thumb to take on the shape of the little mould.

- Once the tray is filled, turn it over onto a flat board with a hard tap, which will release the kunafa pistachio-side up.

Loukoumathes

Makes 25–30

FOR THE SYRUP:
300g caster sugar
400ml water
300g jar clear Greek honey
3 pieces of cinnamon bark

FOR THE BATTER:
800g plain flour
1 tsp. salt
1 tsp. dried yeast
Lukewarm water
Groundnut oil, for deep frying

Across Greece and the Levant, street vendors sell their own variation of these deliciously sweet honey fritters. There is nothing like the aroma of freshly made Loukoumathes to draw in the crowds. And when making these at home, I struggle to keep up with the family waiting for the next fritter to come out of the pan.

- Place all the ingredients for the syrup in a saucepan and bring to a steady boil for 5 minutes, then leave to cool.

- To make the batter, sift the flour and salt into a deep bowl, forming a well in the centre. Dissolve the yeast in a tablespoon of lukewarm water and pour into the well. Bind together while gradually adding enough lukewarm water to form a light batter the consistency of double cream.

- Beat the mixture, then cover with a clean cloth and leave in a warm place to rise. When it has doubled in volume with bubbles appearing on the surface, the batter is ready to use.

- Pour enough oil into a heavy-based deep-lidded pan to fill to one-third. Slowly heat the oil to the correct frying temperature. If you drop a teaspoonful of batter into the hot oil, it will bubble and rise to the surface if hot enough.

- Wet your left hand under cold water then place it in the doughy batter. Squeeze your palm together until a ball of dough pops up appearing by your thumb. Scoop it with a wet teaspoon and carefully drop it into hot oil.

- Keep an eye on the temperature of the oil and continue to fry in batches until you have used up the batter. When the fritters are puffed and golden brown, remove with a slotted spoon and immediately dip in cold syrup. Transfer to a shallow serving plate.

Caramelised Figs with Spiced Yoghurt

Serves 6

300g Greek yoghurt
½ tsp. ground cinnamon
¼ tsp. ground cloves
4 tsp. clear Greek honey
6 large ripe figs
2 tbsp. pistachio nuts,
   coarsely chopped

I love the crunch of seeds in sweet fresh figs, and this recipe is a favourite way to enjoy them, either for breakfast or as a healthy snack anytime of the day. They're quick to make and delicious.

- In a small bowl, mix together the yoghurt, cinnamon and cloves. Sweeten with 2 tsp. honey. Chill until required.

- Halve the figs through the stalk and brush the cut side with a little more honey. Heat a non-stick frying pan and cook the figs cut-side down for 5 minutes or until softened and nicely browned.

- Serve warm onto individual plates cut-side up with a good spoonful of chilled spiced yoghurt and sprinkled with the pistachio nuts.

Rizogalo

Serves around 8–10

175g–200g pudding rice
1 litre full-fat milk
150g caster sugar
6 tbsp. orange blossom water
   or rosewater
3 heaped tbsp. corn flour
Ground cinnamon
Shredded orange peel

Nursery food at its best, although for a grown-up touch, I like to top a bowl of rice with a pear poached in red wine. In the summer months, I flavour the rice with rosewater and decorate with fresh rose petals.

- Place the rice in a large saucepan and pour on enough cold water to cover the rice by about 2.5cm. Cover and cook the rice gently until most of the water has been absorbed. Stir in the milk, gradually bring to the boil then reduce the heat to simmer. Cover and cook for 15–20 minutes.

- Stir the sugar and orange blossom water into the rice. Blend the corn flour with enough milk or water to make a thin paste and stir in, simmering until the mixture thickens.

- Divide the creamy rice between individual bowls or one large serving dish. Leave to cool, then refrigerate for around 2 hours.

- Just before serving, sprinkle with cinnamon and decorate with shavings of orange peel.

Pavlova Greek Yoghurt Sundae

Serves 6

300ml double cream
500g plain Greek yoghurt
3 tbsp. icing sugar, sifted
3 tbs. rosewater
150g raspberries
3–4 small meringue nests, bought
  or homemade
2 tbsp. coarsely crushed
  pistachio nuts
6–8 cubes of loukoumia, halved
  diagonally
Fresh mint, to decorate

A wonderful modern-day twist on our good old-fashioned sundae... made with layers of crisp, light meringue, raspberries, and creamy yoghurt flavoured with rosewater and loukoumia.

- In a large mixing bowl, whip the cream until it forms soft peaks. Fold in the yoghurt, icing sugar and rosewater. Cover and chill until required.

- When ready to serve, fill the bottom half of each glass with raspberries, crumbled meringue and crushed pistachio, in that order.

- Spoon on half of the yoghurt mix, repeat with the raspberry, meringue and nut layer and top with the remaining yoghurt mix.

- Decorate with the loukoumia and a sprig of mint. Serve immediately.

Kitchen note: The word 'loukoumia' roughly translates in Arabic and many of other languages as 'soothes the throat' or 'quiets the voice'. This Greek confectionery, also known as Turkish Delight, is soft and chewy, sugar-sweet and comes in many traditional flavours.

Greek Yoghurt with Walnuts in Syrup

Serves 4

4 Glyko Karydaki from a jar
400g Greek yoghurt, well chilled
Mint leaves, to decorate

Glyko Karydaki, or fresh walnuts preserved in syrup, are one of many different varieties of 'spoon sweets' made in most Greek kitchens. As such there is always a jar or two in the larder.

Traditionally served on small glass plates with a drizzle of its syrup and a dessert fork for eating (despite their name), spoon sweets are offered to visitors as a welcoming gesture, always accompanied with a glass of ice cold water. Karydaki, which means small (or young) walnut, is one of the best Greek traditional spoon sweets, made from baby green walnuts harvested in spring when the outer shell has not become hard. The procedure for making it is a bit labour-intensive, so buy a jar from your local Greek or Middle Eastern deli and enjoy.

- Slice each walnut into 6–8 segments, leaving the walnut in its whole form.

- Spread the yoghurt into a disc onto 4 small serving plates.

- Place a number of walnut wedges to form a neat flower or star shape on top of the yoghurt.

- Drizzle some syrup from the jar around each walnut and decorate with a mint leaf or two.

Stella Stathopoulou

Melomakarona

These honey cookies are one of the most popular treats throughout Greece over the Christmas season. The fragrant aroma from these little egg-shaped cookies fills the house with 'Christmas', bringing back childhood memories.

Makes approx. 30

FOR THE SYRUP:
500ml water
500g granulated sugar
500g clear Greek honey plus
    extra for drizzling
Pared rind from 1 orange
2 cinnamon sticks
10 whole cloves

FOR THE DOUGH:
1.5kg plain flour
2 tsp. baking powder
1 tsp. bicarbonate of soda
    (or baking soda)
250ml orange juice
500ml vegetable oil
250g caster sugar
300ml brandy
Ground cinnamon
75g walnuts, coarsely chopped

- First make the syrup: Place the water, sugar and honey in a saucepan with the orange rind, cinnamon and cloves. Bring to a steady simmer over a medium-high heat to dissolve the sugar, gently bubbling to form a light syrup. Remove from the heat, whisk and set aside to cool.

- Preheat the oven to 180°C (fan 160°C) / Gas 4. Line 2 flat baking sheets with parchment paper.

- For the dough, sift the flour and baking powder into one bowl. In another large bowl, blend the bicarbonate of soda with a little of the orange juice then whisk in the remaining orange juice, vegetable oil, sugar and brandy. Tip the flour onto the liquid mixture and using your hands, gently fold through the mixture to form a smooth dough. Do not over-knead as the mixture can split.

- Using a dessert spoon, take a small amount of dough, then roll into an egg shaped oval 3–4cm long. Arrange evenly onto a baking sheet and cook for 20–25 minutes or until the cookies are dark golden-brown and crisp. Be patient: cook a batch or baking sheet at a time so that the hot cookies can be immediately steeped in the cold syrup whilst another batch is cooking. Using a slotted spoon, immediately dip the hot cookies, 6 or so at a time, into the cold syrup, leave for about 10 seconds, then drain and transfer onto a large shallow serving dish. Repeat with the remaining cookies as soon as they come out of the oven. Hot cookies into cold syrup!

- Drizzle the pile of cookies with some more honey, a sprinkling of ground cinnamon (or cloves) and scatter on the walnuts.

Cocktails

Apollo

Our wonderful Apollo cocktail was created for us by award winning mixologist Antonis Vasiliadis. If it's cocktails you love then our Berwick Street Real Greek is the one for you.

50ml masticha
25ml lemon juice
20ml cardamom syrup
50ml apple juice
25ml egg white
1 sprig of thyme, to garnish

- Put some ice cubes in a shaker.

- Pour in the ingredients except the thyme.

- Shake well and pour into a cocktail glass.

- Garnish with a sprig of thyme

Ouzo mojito

Brown sugar
25ml ouzo
¼ lime
4 mint leaves
Soda water, to top up

- Crush some brown sugar with 3–4 slices of lime and 4–5 leaves of mint and put in a cocktail glass.

- Add some crushed ice.

- Pour in the ouzo and top up with soda water.

- Decorate with a wedge of lime and a sprig of fresh mint and serve with a couple of straws.

Greek Mountain Tea

Also know as ironwort or 'shepherds' tea', the Greeks call their mountain tea 'sideritis', which is literally translated as 'he who is made of or has iron'. Ironwort has been traditionally used to aid digestion, strengthen the immune system and suppress common colds, the flu and other viruses, and help with allergies and shortness of breath, sinus congestion and even pain and mild anxiety. Added to that, it tastes delicious, so you have the perfect herbal tea.

Greek Coffee

You will find coffee like this served all over the Greek and Middle Eastern world. Some call it Turkish coffee, some Egyptian coffee, some Arabic coffee, but as it all started in Greece, we call ours Greek coffee!

Making Greek coffee is an art form and cannot be rushed. If you do, you will not get the 'kaimaki', that frothy cream on the surface, which is the sign of a good coffee.

There are a few ways that you can take your coffee:

Sketo: with no sugar
Medrio: with one sugar
Malo-gliki: one and a half sugars
Gliki: very sweet, with two sugars

In a briki, a specially shaped small pan, traditionally a copper-style pot, you measure out how many coffees you are making using one Greek coffee cupful of water per person.

Add the sugar (unless you are going **'sketo'**) and stir. Now, before the water gets too hot, add a heaped spoonful of good-quality, finely ground coffee for each cup of water, stirring well.

Allow to simmer, then just as it is about to boil, take off the heat and pour the coffee into each cup until three-quarters full, then go back around the cups of coffee to top up with the *'kaimaki'* or frothy cream, so everyone gets their fair share!

Don't forget: You never drink Greek coffee to the bottom as you will end up with a mouthful of bitter sediment!

If you are lucky, Yiayia (grandma) may be around to tip your cup upside down and turn it three times, allowing the sediment to fall, then she will tip it back upright and read your fortune in the patterns left behind.

Suppliers and Produce

Greek Yoghurt

Greek yoghurt is heavily strained to remove the liquid whey and lactose, leaving behind a tangy, creamy product. Plain Greek yoghurt possesses double the protein, half the carbs and half the sodium of the regular variety. It is fortified with essential nutrients and packed with probiotics, which helps with gut health. It's also low in sodium but high in potassium and calcium, and contains B12, which is normally found in meat, so if meat's not your thing, then yoghurt is a great way to add this nutrient to your diet.

Yoghurt really is a wonderfood. It aids in weight management by creating less cortisol, aids digestion and contains many beneficial bacteria. It can boost your immune system and increase bone mass. A little bit can help in so many ways.

It is a staple part of the Greek diet and can be eaten in both a sweet and savoury way. I can't start my day without a dollop of Greek yoghurt, a handful of nuts and a drizzle of Ikarian honey.

Ikarian Honey

Ikaria, located in the eastern Aegean, is named after Ikarus, the son of Dedalus who flew too close to the sun. Ikaria is known as the 'healing island' where people commonly live until their nineties due to a combination of factors involving the food they eat, their lifestyle and their mindset. This is why it's known as the island where people forget to die.

One of the foods they eat regularly is Ikarian honey, a very high-quality product. It is made from many plants: Pine trees, herbs and a variety of native flora species found on the island. Among them are the white heather tree, Greek Strawberry tree, pine tree, wild lavender, Akoniza, thyme and wild oregano.

All these trees and plants hold incredible health benefits; the Ikarians use them for tea as well. The pollen and nectar collected by the bees is 100% pure and free from the chemicals or pesticides/herbicides that are normally found in commercial or private farming. There is no industrialization or large commercial enterprise on the island, which helps avoid pollutants. Every plant here grows naturally and wild, without the use of pesticides or fertilizers. The trees blossom in spring and also in autumn, assuring sustenance for the bees throughout the year. No manpower is needed at all.

The honey itself is medium to dark brown, due mostly to the pine trees. It has a unique, rich flavour marking it out from other honeys and is believed to have anti-cancer, anti-inflammatory and antibacterial properties.

Ikarians are very aware of the honey's medicinal properties, so they eat a spoonful everyday and sometimes add garlic and use it as cough medicine.

Cheese

Greeks have an experiential relationship with cheese. We are, in fact, considered to be its inventors. In his millennia-old book *The Iliad*, Homer describes the cheese produced by the Cyclops Polyphemus; a cheese that is believed to be the ancestor of feta. According to the myth, Polyphemus realized one day, to his surprise, that the milk he collected from his sheep and carried in a utricle (a carrying invention made from an animal's stomach lining), had turned into a solid, tasty food that could be preserved.

Feta cheese is by far the most popular Greek cheese; creamy, rich and tangy, it is a delicious white cheese with a crumbly texture. We source our feta from Epirus, an award-winning cheese manufacturer. Livestock in Epirus yields the richest and most aromatic milk for the production of feta. This is due to the unique flora of the region, which includes an endless variety of grasses and herbs that grow both by the sea and in its high mountains. This high-quality, flavoursome milk meets with the cheese-making skills of the people of Epirus to result in a feta that stands out for its racy flavour and special aroma.

Halloumi cheese originated in Cyprus in the Medieval Byzantine period and subsequently became popular throughout the Middle East. Halloumi has made a classic British culinary journey from ethnic specialty to commonplace item. Its charms have long been recognized in its homeland of Cyprus, where the average resident gets through an average of 8kg (17lbs) of it each year. Now Britons are said to consume more halloumi than any other European country outside Cyprus.

Olive Oil

The saying goes 'if you cut a Greek open you will find olive oil running in their veins'. Olive oil is, without a shadow of a doubt, the elixir of life in Greece.

Four decades ago, researchers from the Seven Countries Study concluded that the monounsaturated fats in olive oil were largely responsible for the low rates of heart disease and cancer on the Greek island of Crete. Now we know that olive oil also contains polyphenols, powerful antioxidants that may help prevent age-related diseases.

Olive oil is the cornerstone of the Greek diet – an essential nutritional mainstay for the world's longest-living culture. Apparently, the average Greek consumes 23 litres of olive oil a year. The health benefits of olive oil are unrivalled and research reveals more benefits nearly every day. In fact, we are only just beginning to understand the countless ways in which olive oil can improve our health, and our lives.

Here at The Real Greek, we use the best Cretan olive oil sourced from an award-winning family run company called Latzimas.

Wine

Wine has been an important part of Greek culture for thousands of years, as the numerous archaeological discoveries throughout the country have revealed. The ancient Greeks knew well the nutritional value and enjoyment of wine, as it became an inseparable part of their daily life.

The ancient Greeks pioneered new methods of viticulture and wine production that they shared with early winemaking communities in what are now France, Italy, Austria and Russia, as well as others, through trade and colonization. Along the way, they markedly influenced the ancient European winemaking cultures of the Celts, Etruscans, Scythians and, ultimately, the Romans.

At The Real Greek, we work with the best wine producers Greece has to offer. Tsantali Wines are one such producer. Their vineyard has always been the core of the Tsantali philosophy. The rejuvenation of some of the most exquisite vineyards in Northern Greece like Mount Athos, Rapsani, Halkidiki and Maronia, is attributed to the family's vision. Thanks to the Tsantalis' dedication and strategic investment, today outstanding traditions are safely kept, biodiversity and native grapes are preserved and incentives have been given to younger vine growers and winemakers. This long-standing heritage is carried on today by the third and fourth Tsantali generation.

Cookoovaya

The Real Greek is about everything authentically Greek – people, knowledge and flavours. It is very proud to maintain strong ties with the best chefs of Athens, who came for one night only to our flagship Bankside Restaurant to share the **Cookoovaya** Wise Cuisine experience with the UK audience. Five renowned Greek chefs, each distinguished for a specific talent, joined forces to create **Cookoovaya**, a celebration of modern Greek cuisine using only the finest ingredients Greece has to offer.

Spyros and **Vangelis Liakos** are famous for the realization of the best meat restaurant in Athens: **Base Grill**. Knowledge, passion, perseverance and curiosity led them to, tenderly, approach meat as a work of art. They take pride in choosing the type of meat and the cut, and they assess each piece to ensure that it is perfectly prepared. They source their meat from all over Greece from amazing heritage-breed pigs and cattle, including the most spectacular 100-day-hung steak. **Pericles Koskinas** began travelling the kitchens of the world to visit the best restaurants, such as **Milos**. He is not only creating new plates, but keeps an eye on everything, like a true manager.

Nikos Karathanos, twice awarded with a Michelin star, believes that passion about wise cuisine should be boundless.

Kleomenis Zournatzis monitors global changes and trends in an attempt to comprehend and communicate the essence of food as he perceives it.

Together, the collective venture of these chefs, **Cookoovaya**, is the epitome of seasonal modern Greek cuisine, taking the finest Greek ingredients and preparing them in the most flavoursome and innovative ways.

The Real Greek Dips and Meze

Greek eating is all about meze, and you can't have meze without dips. In the book are the recipes for all our dips, but also coming soon to all good supermarkets will be The Real Greek authentic meze and dips.

Taramasalata: Rich, creamy dip made from cod roe. It's not meant to be pink!

Spicy Feta Dip (Htipiti): Real Greek feta cheese with roasted peppers and a chilli kick.

Melitzanosalata: A blend of aubergines, spring onions and olive oil flavoured with garlic and a hint of parsley.

Tzatziki: Cool and tangy Greek yoghurt with cucumber and garlic.

Houmous: A blend of chickpeas and sesame seed paste flavoured with garlic.

Index

(page numbers in italic type refer to photographs)

Acknowledgements

Nabil and Tonia would like to thank all of our Real Greek family for all of their hard work and dedication in making The Real Greek what it is today.

http://www.therealgreek.com/